THE TERRY LECTURES

# Absence of Mind

## THE DISPELLING
## OF INWARDNESS
## FROM THE MODERN MYTH
## OF THE SELF

*Other Volumes in the Terry Lecture Series Available from Yale*

# *Absence of* Mind

THE DISPELLING

OF INWARDNESS

FROM THE MODERN MYTH

OF THE SELF

*Marilynne Robinson*

Yale UNIVERSITY PRESS

NEW HAVEN & LONDON

Designed by Mary Valencia
Set in Minion type by Keystone Typesetting, Inc.
Printed in the United States of America.

Library of Congress Cataloging-in-Publication Data
Robinson, Marilynne.
Absence of mind : the dispelling of inwardness from the modern myth of
the self / Marilynne Robinson.
p. cm.
Essays from the lectures delivered at Yale University, the
Dwight Harrington Terry Foundation.
Includes bibliographical references.
ISBN 978-0-300-14518-2 (cloth : alk. paper)
1. Religion and science. 2. Philosophy, Modern. 3. Thought and thinking.
I. Dwight Harrington Terry Foundation. II. Title.
BL241.R58 2010
201′.65—dc22 2009044020

A catalogue record for this book is available from the British Library.

This paper meets the requirements of ANSI/NISO Z39.48-1992
(Permanence of Paper).

10   9   8   7   6   5   4   3   2   1

# CONTENTS

These essays examine one side in the venerable controversy called the conflict between science and religion, in order to question the legitimacy of the claim its exponents make to speak with the authority of science and in order to raise questions about the quality of thought that lies behind it. I propose that the model from which these writers proceed is science as the word was understood by certain influential thinkers in the early modern period, the late nineteenth century and the first half of the twentieth century. While it is true that at the same time and in the same culture a new and truly modern physics and cosmology were emerging, both are conspicuous by their absence, then as now, from the arguments of these self-declared champions of science, reason, and enlightenment. The very limited terms that are treated by them as appropriate to the subject around which the controversy has always turned, the origins and nature of our species, inevitably yield a conception of humanity that is itself very limited, excluding as it must virtually all observation and speculation on this subject that have been offered through the ages by those outside the closed circle that is called modern thought.

It is clear that there is a generous element of the arbitrary in the stance assumed by these self-declared rationalists. If one were to say "Either God created the universe, or the universe is a product and consequence of the laws of physics," it might be objected that these two statements are not incompatible, that neither precludes the other. But the second is conventionally taken to preclude the first. So, for purposes of argument, let us say it does, and that the origins of the universe can be taken to be devoid of theological implication. Likewise, if evolution is not to be reconciled with faith, as many religious people as well as many scientists believe, then let us say, again for purposes of argument, that complex life is simply another instance of matter working through the permutations available to it.

These two points being granted, is there more to say

than that existence, stripped of myth, unhallowed and un-haunted, is simply itself? Are there other implications? This starlit world is still the world, presumably, and every part of it, including humankind, is unchanged in its nature, still embodying the history that is also its ontogeny. Surely no rationalist would dispute this. Some might argue that life, absent myth, would be freed of certain major anxieties and illusions, and hostilities as well, but such changes would not touch our essential selves, formed as they have been through biological adaptation.

There is no reason to suppose that arriving at truth would impoverish experience, however it might change the ways in which our gifts and energies are deployed. So nothing about our shared ancestry with the ape can be thought of as altering the fact that human beings are the creators of history and culture. If "mind" and "soul" are not entities in their own right, they are at least terms that have been found useful for describing aspects of the expression and self-experience of our very complex nervous system. The givens of our nature, that we are brilliantly creative and as brilliantly destructive, for example, would persist as facts to be dealt with, even if the word "primate" were taken to describe us exhaustively. I am aware that certain writers have made the argument, or at least the assertion, that conflict arises out of religion and more especially out of religious difference. They would do well to consult Herodotus, or to read up on the career of Napoleon. Extrapolations from contemporary events proceed from far too narrow a base to support a global statement of this kind. And this thesis about the origins of conflict is novel in the long history of the debate over human origins, which has typically argued that conflict is natural to us, as it is to animals, and is, if not good in any ordinary sense, at least necessary to our biological enhancement. However, if attributing conflict to religion, thereby removing hostility and violence from a Darwinist or even a Freudian frame of interpretation, is a departure from tradition, it is at least familiar as a strategy that preserves a favored conclusion by recruiting whatever rationalization might seem to support it. Religion has always been the foil for this tradition, sometimes deplored as the sponsor of dysgenic compassion, sometimes as fomenter of oppression and violence.

Modernist or rationalist arguments are not harmonious with one another, except in their conclusion, which clearly exists in anticipation of its various justifications. This conclusion is, very briefly, that positivism is correct in excluding from the model of reality whatever science is (or was) not competent to verify or falsify. While this view has merits in certain circumstances, it has become encysted within an old polemic, and though it is deeply influential in shaping the posture in the controversy that is called modern and scientific, it has failed to develop and has become in effect the blighted twin of modern science. Positivism was intended to banish the language of metaphysics as meaningless, and it supplied in its place a systematically reductionist conceptual vocabulary, notably in the diverse interpretations of human nature it seemed to endorse. There is simply no way to reconcile the world view of Darwin with that of Freud, or either of these with the theories of Marx or Nietzsche or B. F. Skinner. The one thing they do have in common is the assumption that the Western understanding of what a human being is has been fundamentally in error. This understanding has been based to a great degree on religious narrative and doctrine, and religion has been the subject of their explicit rejection. But the classical and humanist traditions, also deeply influential in Western thought, are just as effectively excluded by these variously determinist and reductionist models of human nature and motivation.

Consider the notion of the human being as microcosm, as a small epitome of the universe. This idea persisted from the beginning of philosophic thought to the beginning of the modern scientific period. In the thought of Heraclitus, we are of one substance with the fire that is the essence of the cosmos. Monads being for Leibniz the fundamental constituents of the cosmos, we are in his scheme a kind of monad whose special character it is to mirror the universe. Through its many variations, the idea of the microcosm asserted a profound kinship between humankind and the whole of being, which common sense must encourage us to believe does in fact exist. It would be more than miraculous, indeed an argument for something like a special creation, if we were in any sense set apart from being as a whole. Our energies can only derive from, and express, the larger phenomenon of energy. And there is that haunting compatibility of our means of knowing with the universe of things to be known. Yet, even as our capacity to describe the fabric of reality and the dimensions of it has undergone an astonishing deepening and expansion, we have turned away from the ancient intuition that we are a part of it all. What such a recognition might imply, if it were attempted on the basis of present knowledge, it is difficult to say, but the strange ways of quarks and photons might enlarge our sense of the mysterious nature of our own existence. The pull of reductionism might be balanced by a countervailing force.

The very truncated model of human being offered by writers in the tradition that has dominated the discussion from the beginning of the modern period is a clear consequence of the positivist rejection of metaphysics. It is true that philosophical speculation was the only means at hand for the old tradition that pondered such ideas as human-soul-as-microcosm. Nevertheless, the insight that we, along with the apes, participate in a reality vastly larger than the sublunary world of hunting and gathering, mating, territorialism, and so on is indisputable. Granting evolution, its materials can only have been the stuff in which a brilliant complexity would have inhered since long before the first generation of stars, to choose a date at random. It is not to be imagined that the character of matter would not profoundly affect the forms in which our reality has emerged.

It is historically accidental that the metaphysics that dealt with our being at this scale was theology or looked like it, and that religion was considered the adversary of true understanding. An attempt to re-integrate us into our cosmic setting might look like theology, or mysticism. If this should be the case, it would be in large part a consequence of the fact that the subject has been allowed to atrophy, and those who take it up again might well be driven back on an old vocabulary. This could be mildly embarrassing, after the long crusade of de-mythification. But such considerations ought not to determine the course of science.

There is another sense in which the modern conversation is truncated. If human nature is the subject that rises when our origins are at issue, then whatever we can know of our past is surely germane, and ill-founded generalizations are at best a distraction to be guarded against. That historical data, the record we have made of our tenure on this planet, should be left out of account may reflect the schism in Western intellectual life that has alienated science and humane learning. But the schism itself has origins in the rejection by positivism and by influential voices in early modern science of the terms in which so much thought and collective memory have been interpreted and recorded.

An associated phenomenon is the notion that we know all we need to know when we have acquainted ourselves with a few simple formulae. We have been optimized by competition and environment, we are shaped by economic forces and means of production, we are inheritors of a primal guilt, we are molded by experiences of frustration and reinforcement. These are all assertions that have shaped modern thought. But they are not to be reconciled with one another. The Freudian neurasthenic is not the Darwinian primate, who is not the Marxist proletarian, who is not the behaviorists' organism available to being molded by a regime of positive and negative sensory experience. To acknowledge an element of truth in each of these models is to reject the claims of descriptive sufficiency made by all of them. What they do have in common, beside the claim to sufficiency, is an exclusion of the testimonies of culture and history. These primary assertions make other information either irrelevant or subordinate to kinds of explanation that serve the favored theory. What is art? It is a means of attracting mates, even though artists may have felt that it was an exploration of experience, of the possibilities of communication, and of the extraordinary collaboration of eye and hand. The old conquerors may have meant to fling themselves against the barricades of fate and mortality, but in fact, through all that misery and disruption, they were really just trying to attract mates. The Freudian self is necessarily frustrated in its desires, and therefore it generates art and culture as a sort of ectoplasm, a sublimation of forbidden impulses. So, it would seem, the first thing to know about art, whatever the account of its motives and origins, is that its maker is self-deceived. Leonardo and Rembrandt may have thought they were competent inquirers in their own right, but we moderns know better.

Recently I read to a class of young writers a passage from Emerson's "The American Scholar" in which he says, "In silence, in steadiness, in severe abstraction, let him hold by himself; add observation to observation, patient of neglect, patient of reproach, and bide his own time,—happy enough if he can satisfy himself alone that this day he has seen something truly. . . . For the instinct is sure, that prompts him to tell his brother what he thinks. He then learns that in going down into the secrets of his own mind he has descended into the secrets of all minds." These words caused a certain perturbation. The self is no longer assumed to be a thing to be approached with optimism, or to be trusted to see anything truly. Emerson is describing the great paradox and privilege of human selfhood, a privilege foreclosed when the mind is trivialized or thought to be discredited. The clutch of certitudes that, together, trivialize and discredit are very much in need of being looked at again.

# ONE

# *On Human Nature*

The mind, whatever else it is, is a constant of everyone's experience, and, in more and other ways than we know, the creator of the reality that we live within, that we live by and for and despite, and that, often enough, we die from. Nothing is more essential to us. In this chapter I wish to draw attention to the character of the thinking that is brought to bear by contemporary writers on the subject, and also to a first premise of modern and contemporary thought, the notion that we as a culture have crossed one or another threshold of knowledge or realization that gives the thought that follows it a special claim to the status of truth. Instances I have chosen to present this case are necessarily few, but in this remarkably reiterative literature they may fairly be called typical.

There is at present an assertive popular literature that describes the mind as if from the posture of science. For the purposes of these writers, it is as if chaste and rational scientific objectivity certified the value of their methods and the truth of their conclusions. The foil for their argument, sometimes implicit, usually explicit, is that old romantic myth of the self still encouraged by religion or left in its wake as a sort of cultural residue needing to be swept away. I have no opinion about the likelihood that science, at the top of its bent, will ultimately arrive at accounts of consciousness, identity, memory, and imagination that are sufficient in the terms of scientific inquiry. Nor do I object, in our present very limited state of knowledge, to hypotheses being offered in the awareness that, in the honorable tradition of science, they are liable to being proved grossly wrong. What I wish to question are not the methods of science, but the methods of a kind of argument that claims the authority of science or highly specialized knowledge, that assumes a protective coloration that allows it to pass for science yet does not practice the self-discipline or self-criticism for which science is distinguished.

These sociologists and evolutionary psychologists and

philosophers carry on an honorable tradition, though in a radically declined form. Indeed, a great part of the excitement of life in the post-Enlightenment period has come with the thought that reality could be reconceived, that knowledge would emancipate humankind if only it could be made accessible to them. Such great issues, human origins and human nature, have the public as an appropriate theater, since the change they propose is cultural. This being the case, however, it is surely incumbent upon writers who undertake to shape opinion to resist the temptation to popularize in the negative sense of that word. Vast and contentious literatures lie behind psychology, anthropology, and sociology. But the popularizers in these fields now are highly regarded figures whom a nonspecialist might reasonably trust to deal competently with the great subjects their books take on, which include human nature and consciousness, and, with striking frequency, religion. The degree of fundamental consensus among these writers is important to their influence.

A model that shapes contemporary writing across any number of fields is the crossing of the threshold. It asserts that the world of thought, recently or in an identifiable moment in the near past, has undergone epochal change. Some realization has intervened in history with miraculous abruptness and efficacy, and everything is transformed. This is a pattern that recurs very widely in the contemporary world of ideas. I pick up a slender volume of philosophy and read as follows: "In this post-modern condition, faith, no longer modeled on the Platonic image of the motionless God, absorbs these dualisms [theism and atheism] without recognizing in them any reasons for conflict."[1] Here we have news of the explosion of an assumption—Western religion was modeled on a pagan conception of God as "motionless," until postmodern hermeneutics intervened.

Then what is Western religion? Apparently nothing I have come across in my nonspecialist perusals of the theology of the past five hundred years. If the Unmoved Mover, whom I take to be the subject here, imparted motion to the created order, is it meaningful to call him "motionless," which sounds very like "static" or "inert," and is not consistent with the great and ancient intuition brilliantly understood as the imparting of motion? An early Christian writer, Gregory of Nyssa, said of God, "That which is without quality cannot be measured, the invisible cannot be examined, the incorporeal cannot be weighed, the limitless cannot be compared, the incomprehensible does not admit of more or less."[2] From antiquity, insistence on the ontological unlikeness of God to the categories to which the human mind has recourse is at the center of theological reflection. What cannot be measured or compared clearly cannot be unmoved in any ordinary sense of that word. This is exactly the kind of language positivism finds meaningless, though in its reaching beyond accustomed categories embedded in language it resembles nothing so much as contemporary physics. In any case, did this idea of a motionless God, whether the understanding of it was complex or simple, continue to influence faith until the very recent arrival of the "postmodern condition"? What are believed by some to have been assumptions powerful enough to shape the culture of a civilization, and to reshape it by their demise, have been for many others no assumptions at all.

The paradigm for narrative of this kind is based on the idea of the historical threshold—before we thought thus, and now, in this new age of comprehension, we, or the enlightened among us, think otherwise. There are any number of thresholds, which initiate any number of new conceptual eras. And in every case there is a statement about the past, as seen from the vantage of a fundamentally altered present. In the philosophy books I find sentences like this one: "This hermeneuticization of philosophy freed religion from metaphysics at the moment when it had identified the death of God, announced by Nietzsche, with the death of Christ on the cross narrated by the Gospels."[3] Nietzsche, and some phrases that are identified with him, notably this one and

"There are no facts, only interpretations," often figure as threshold events in these metanarratives, as they appear to do in this case.

It would be helpful to the general reader if such books were to provide definitions of major terms. To define Western Christianity is no easy thing, granted, considering the very prolonged history of conflict and schism within Christianity. I have quoted from the preface to *The Future of Religion* by Richard Rorty and Gianni Vattimo. It is a good-hearted, even rather joyful book that announces the passage of Western Christianity from a law of power through its Nietzschean moment to an embrace of the law of love. I am eager to welcome the first sign of the reality of this transformation. Still, I suspect no attempt at a definition of Western Christianity would arrive at a place where generalization would be possible, and I suspect therefore that definition may be avoided here as elsewhere in order to permit generalization.

*The Future of Religion* is a departure from other books I will mention in that it takes religion to have a future of a kind, and the world to be better for the fact. The transformation of God from a figure of awe and fear to a force of love immanent in humankind grants him being, realized through consensus of belief. This looks to me like the sort of thing William James might call a monism, a Hegelism.[4] How exactly is such a consensus reached? Let us say historic change does occur in that thinly populated upper atmosphere where a phrase of Nietzsche's matters, where the "deconstruction of metaphysics" has consequence. How is it lived in the hundreds of millions of minds who might actualize this consensus? These questions are not meant to invoke any sort of populist standard, as if I were to say, "The man on the street may be wholly unaware that metaphysics has been deconstructed, and might not approve the project if he were aware of it." No, quite the opposite. They are meant to call to mind the voice of the Psalmist, the voice of any ancient poet, saint, or visionary on the far side of the threshold who has attested to his or her own sense of the holy, and all those who are moved by these voices and attest to the truth of them.

This goes to the very nature of religion. James defined religion as the "feelings, acts and experiences of individual men in their solitude, so far as they apprehend themselves to stand in relation to whatever they may consider the divine."[5] The words "solitude" and "individual" are crucial here, since this is the unvarying condition of the mind, no matter the web of culture and language by which it is enabled, sustained, and limited. The thing lost in this kind of thinking, the kind that proposes a "moment" in which religion is freed by "hermeneuticization," is the self, the solitary, perceiving, and interpreting locus of anything that can be called experience. It may have been perverse of destiny to array perception across billions of subjectivities, but the fact is central to human life and language and culture, and no philosophy or cognitive science should be allowed to evade it.

Where a definition of religion is attempted in this literature, it tends to be of the kind tentatively proposed by Daniel Dennett, who describes religions as "social systems whose participants avow belief in a supernatural agent or agents whose approval is to be sought." The book I have in hand is Dennett's *Breaking the Spell: Religion as a Natural Phenomenon*. Dennett says his definition of religion is "profoundly at odds with that of William James," the one I have quoted. He rejects the definition on the grounds that it describes "individuals who very sincerely and devoutly take themselves to be the lone communicants of what we might call private religions," and on these grounds "I shall call them spiritual people, but not religious." Note that religion is singular in James's definition and plural in Dennett's. James is describing an experience that he takes to be universal among religions of all descriptions, while Dennett sees religions as distinct "social systems." The insistence in Dennett's writing on the demographics of religion, on what, by his lights, is observable and therefore accessible to science as he understands it, recalls Bertrand Russell's remark that "it is the privacy of introspective data which causes much of the behaviourists' objection to them." Bertrand Russell was writing as a critic of behaviorism in 1921, but behaviorism is a branch of psychology that seems to have passed out of style without taking its major assumptions along with it, so his comment is still to the point.[6]

Dennett sheers off the contemplative side of faith, its subjectivity, as if the collective expressions of religion and the inward experience of it were nonoverlapping magisteria, as if religion were only what could be observed using the methods of anthropology or of sociology, without reference to the deeply pensive solitudes that bring individuals into congregations and communities to be nurtured by the thought and culture they find there. Thus is he freed to bypass John Donne and the Sufi poets and to move on to a description of the practices of cargo cultists, whom, it is unfortunately fair to assume, anthropology does not present in the richest light, either. For the moment it is sufficient to point out that the religious experiences James describes in his *Varieties of Religious Experience* are attested to as the subjective experience of individuals who are in fact associated with denominations. Their experiences are of a kind reported, especially in America, through both Great Awakenings and long after them. These individuals are hardly lone communicants of private religions.

What an interesting problem is being evaded here! The great quarrel in modern Western life is said to be between religion and science. They tend to be treated as if there were a kind of symmetry between them, presumably because of their supposed Manichean opposition. But science is a comparatively recent phenomenon, for several centuries strongly identified with the culture of the West, which it has profoundly influenced and by which it has been formed and channeled. Because it is recent and culturally localized, it is difficult to distinguish from its setting. Certainly modern warfare, hot and cold, has had a profound impact on the development of science in the same period that science has had its most profound impact on human life. Nuclear energy and the Internet are two cases in point.

Religion, on the contrary, is ancient and global, and, since it has no clear geographic or temporal limits, persisting as cultural habit even where it seems to have been suppressed or renounced, it is very difficult to define, "definition" being a word which means etymologically and in fact "a setting of limits." Christianity as a subset of religion is associated in its origins and its spread with a historical period and with particular regions and populations. And yet, fractal-like, it seems to replicate the complexities of the larger phenomenon. Bertrand Russell, distinguished mathematician, philosopher, and despiser of religion and Christianity, said, "At all times, from the age of Constantine to the end of the seventeenth century, Christians were far more fiercely persecuted by other Christians than they ever were by the Roman emperors."[7] No Christian with even a sectarian sense of history would dispute this, since every sect has its own tale of persecution. And most acknowledge that they—the tradition with which they identify—have at some time engaged in it. But if the Roman emperors martyred fewer Christians than the Christians, their relative numbers in the population are certainly relevant here—the emperors presided over a remarkably brutal society, brilliant as it was. As is usual, Russell blames Christian violence on the traditions of Jewish monotheism, not on the norms of the pagan civilization in which the faith took root.

Still, it is true that religions differ less from the world at large than one might hope. And yet the fact that conflict occurs along national and demographic lines that are sometimes also religious lines cannot be assumed to mean that the issue or motivation of the conflict is religion. Not long before Russell spoke, Christian Europe had been engulfed in a terrible war whose causes seem to have been secular ones— the fears and ambitions of rival states and empires. It is seldom if ever the case that religious considerations are determinants in such matters. This adds another dimension to the difficulty of defining religion.

\*

Russell means to refute the argument that religion raises the moral level of civilization, a defense the religious do offer.

The atheist regimes of the French Revolution and of the twentieth century may come as near providing a point of comparison as there has ever been, and they hardly argue in favor of this view. But there is no point quibbling. If the Christianity Russell loathes is the Christianity he encountered, then that is a form in which the religion has lived in the world. Others have encountered other Christianities. This is one more instance of the universe of difficulties that surrounds a definition of one religion, not to mention religion as a whole. Nevertheless, it is odd to see a controversy rage at the center of the civilization over so many generations, at least half of it the impassioned work of self-declared rationalists, and to find so little attempt at a definition of major terms, beyond the polemical kind of definition that guarantees one position the satisfactions of finding itself true and right.

I linger over this because religion is indisputably a central factor in any account of the character and workings of the human mind. Does religion manifest a capacity for deep insight, or an extraordinary proneness to delusion? Both, perhaps, like the mind itself. In 1927, in the course of refuting the classical arguments for the existence of God, Russell dealt with the belief in a Creator in these terms: "There is no reason to suppose that the world had a beginning at all. The idea that things must have a beginning is really due to the poverty of our imagination. Therefore, perhaps, I need not waste any more time upon the argument about the First Cause."[8] From a scientific standpoint, this was a perfectly reputable statement at the time he made it. Then, two years later, Edwin Hubble made observations that were understood to imply the universe is expanding, and the modern narrative of beginnings emerged, that more-than-explosive imparting of motion. No one need be persuaded to belief by the fact that things did indeed come into being, or that their genesis, so to speak, seems to have been as abrupt as Genesis says it was. Still, Russell's science was in error. In the great matter of beginnings, so germane to the nature of being, many "primitive" or classical religions have had a sounder intuition. If this fact has no force as evidence of human insight, it is still impressive in its own uninterpretable right. That ancient minds pondered cosmic origins should inspire a little awe for what human beings are, what the mind is.

I did not plan to give particular attention to religion here. I intended to cite Bertrand Russell and John Searle, both nonreligious, in support of my argument that the mind as felt experience had been excluded from important fields of modern thought. I meant to restrict myself, more or less, to looking at the characteristic morphology of the otherwise very diverse schools of modern thought for which the mind/ brain is a subject. But I find that these schools are themselves engrossed with religion—as problem, as anomaly, or as adversary—to a degree that makes the subject unavoidable. When faith is described as an element in culture and history, its nature tends to be grossly simplified, despite the vast and unconsulted literature of religious thought and testimony. It would surely be difficult to condescend to religion when it is articulate in terms that are accessible to Western understanding. An honest inquirer into its nature might spend an afternoon listening to Bach or Palestrina, reading Sophocles or the Book of Job.

Instead, religion is a point of entry for certain anthropological methods and assumptions whose tendencies are distinctly invidious. It is treated as a proof of persisting primitivity among human beings that legitimizes the association of all religion with the lowest estimate Europeans have made of aboriginal practices, and legitimizes also the assumption that humankind is itself fearful, irrational, deluded, and self-deceived, excepting, of course, these missionaries of enlightenment. If there is an agenda behind the implicit and explicit polemic against religion, which is now treated as brave and new, now justified by Wahhabism and occasional eruptions of creationist zeal, but is fully present in the rationalism of the eighteenth century, it may well be that it creates rhetorical occasions for asserting an anthropology of modern humanity, a hermeneutics of condescension.

To condescend effectively it is clearly necessary to adhere to a narrow definition of relevant data. The existence of God and the ways in which his existence might be apprehended have formed an old and very rich conversation among sects and nations. That God or the gods might be hidden or absent is a recurring trope in religious literatures. The pious have seen the world as if empty of a divine presence and pondered the experience at length. Saints have had their dark nights and testified to them. It was Luther who wrote about the Deus Absconditus and the death of God as well, and Bonhoeffer who gave Grotius's *etsi Deus non daretur* a new theological application.[9] The characterization of religion by those who dismiss it tends to reduce it to a matter of bones and feathers and wishful thinking, a matter of rituals and social bonding and false etiologies and the fear of death, and this makes its persistence very annoying to them. Then there is the fact that it does persist, and here in America, a country as modern as any, except in this crucial regard. Further grounds for annoyance.

Bertrand Russell says, "Language sometimes conceals the complexity of a belief. We say that a person believes in God, and it might seem as if God formed the whole content of the belief. But what is really believed is that God exists, which is far from being simple. . . . In like manner all cases where the content of a belief seems simple at first sight will be found, on examination, to confirm the view that the content is always complex."[10] This good atheist, despite his contempt for religion, proceeds by introspection, by observation of the processes of his own mind as a means of understanding the human mind, and with a delight in the workings of language he assumes his audience is bright enough to share. His rejection of religion is real and deep, but he does not justify it at the cost of failing to acknowledge the intrinsic complexity of human subjectivity, whatever its specific content. To acknowledge this is to open the archives of all that humankind has thought and done, to see how the mind describes itself, to weigh the kind of evidence supposed science tacitly disallows.

\*

The adventitious use of the idea of "the primitive" seems always to involve the questionable use of questionable information. In *The Blank Slate: The Modern Denial of Human Nature,* Steven Pinker debunks belief in the soul, that is, the Ghost in the Machine, as well as the Noble Savage and, in his view the most persistent of erroneous conceptions of the self, the Blank Slate. He takes all these terms to be simple and naive in a degree that is hardly consistent with the seriousness of the philosophic traditions from which they emerged. By human nature Pinker means the genetically determined factors in behavior, which he takes to be highly significant and broadly unappreciated. In his discussion of the notion of the Noble Savage, he offers a graph comparing male deaths caused by warfare in the twentieth century. The graph is presented as evidence that this rate of mortality among Europeans and Americans, as a percentage of deaths, is minuscule beside those reported among various contemporary "pre-state societies" who would have been the primitives of earlier studies. On the facing page Pinker has noted the errors of Margaret Mead in Samoa and the staged discovery of the "gentle Tasaday." This is worth noting because two bars on his graph represent two subgroups of the Yanomamo, a society whose violent tendencies were the discovery of an anthropological venture whose reports have also been considered suspect. Since his argument is a rejection of "the image of peaceable, egalitarian and ecology-loving natives," an argument that would certainly incline him to welcome information to the effect that these pre-stateans are indeed violent, it would be reassuring to see a slightly more even-handed use of evidence. It would be reassuring also to see some note taken of the susceptibility of such observations to hoaxing and manipulation that has been made so clear in the matter of the Tasaday, the Samoans, and, quite possibly, the Yanomamo, together with an acknowledgment that those who use such observations are susceptible in turn to over-valuing data that tend to confirm them in their views.[11]

Other questions arise. What is meant by warfare? Would

its victims include the millions killed in the regions of Africa from which rubber was taken for use by the armies of World War I? Or are only European and American casualties counted? Does colonialism itself fall outside the definition of warfare, presumably on the grounds that only one side has effective weapons? Should this reckoning exclude the non-male deaths at the siege of Stalingrad or the fall of Berlin? If the point at issue here is how prone societies are to engage in lethal violence, then male mortality caused by warfare is clearly too narrow a category to be meaningful. This is true even putting aside the fact that these pre-state people lack written records, and that traditional narratives of warfare tend to grossly exaggerate the numbers involved in it.

And is it not a little preposterous to make comparisons like this one on the basis of percentages when there are such radical differences in the sizes of these populations? Pinker notes that "two deaths in a band of fifty people is the equivalent of ten million deaths in a country the size of the United States."[12] Is this a meaningful statement? Any extended family with twenty-five members suffers a death from time to time. Is this in any way equivalent to the loss of five million people out of the whole population? The destruction of ten million people would require a prolonged and determined campaign of violence mounted by societies that were equipped to carry it out—not unthinkable, given the history of the Western world. It would mean that the methods required to engage in violence on such a scale would have to have been in readiness, as we all know they are. Does this reflect at all on our pre-dispositions? More to the point, deaths in a band of fifty could never fall below two percent, while the United States could lose two and a half million people and not exceed one percent, which, by this style of reckoning, would make us the less violent society. And why are we comparing a male war party to the entire population of the United States in any case?

Finally, is it reasonable to debunk the myth of the Noble Savage by pondering any twentieth-century society, however remote and exotic? We can have no knowledge of their history, so we cannot know if what appears to us as primitivity is not dispossession and marginalization. Pinker himself notes that some kind of cultural impoverishment happened among the Tasmanians after they migrated from Australia.[13] I hold no particular brief for the notion of primal innocence, yet neither am I content to see so defective a case made against it. But the point of the graph Pinker uses to illustrate his argument is to make a statement about essential human nature, to tell us what we are, to propose an answer to as grave a query as we can make of ourselves, an answer leveraged against highly questionable data presented as if it had the authority of scientific objectivity behind it.

There is a slackness that is pervasively characteristic of

this important conversation. I incline to attribute it to the myth of the threshold I mentioned earlier, the notion that, after Darwin, after Nietzsche, after Freud, after structuralism and post-structuralism, after Crick and Watson and the death of God, some assumptions were to be regarded as fixed and inevitable and others as exposed for all time and for all purposes as naive and untenable, supplanted by a better understanding. Galileo is invoked often. In denominating any moment in history, whether real or imagined, as the threshold moment, a writer or school is asserting a prerogative, the right to characterize the past and establish the terms in which discourse will be conducted from this point forward. Some transformative concept has obliged us to rethink the world in its new light, assuming pervasive error in previous thought and its survivals. The flood of neologisms into certain disciplines seems meant to signal radical departure. Since Darwinism is an important model for many writers in this style, one might expect the evolution of culture to have a place in their worldview. But this transformation they describe is like saltation so complete as to have leapt free of genetic inheritance. In culture as in nature there is no leaving the past behind, but to have done so, to have stepped over a threshold that separates old error from new insight, is the given from which these schools of thought proceed, as posture and as method. Triumphalism was never the friend of

reason. And the tone of too many of these books is patron-
izing. Still, however these writers regard their readers, as
bringers of truth to those who sit in darkness they should act
on their stated devotion to intellectual rigor.

I was educated to believe that a threshold had indeed
been crossed in the collective intellectual experience, that we
had entered a realm called "modern thought," and we must
naturalize ourselves to it. We had passed through a door that
could swing only one way. Major illusions had been dispelled
for good and all. What we had learned from Darwin, Marx,
Freud, and others were insights into reality so deep as to be
ahistorical. Criticism was nostalgia, and skepticism meant
the doubter's mind was closed and fearful. To an age of
doubt this ought to have seemed a naive response to any
body of thought. But these ideas presented themselves as the
last word in doubt, the nec plus ultra of intellectual skepticism. And so they have been regarded for generations,
achieving a remarkable pertinacity through their association
with epochal, and oddly immutable, change. There have always been new interpretations budding off from these seminal works, themselves budding off again and again, revisions
of various sorts typically announcing with the prefix "neo-"
their claim on the world's attention, and at the same time
their undiminished fealty to the school from which they
might otherwise be seen to depart. The prefix "post-" sig-

nifies, of course, that they have crossed some sort of threshold, and can therefore make some new claim on the world's attention.

The schools of thought that support the modernist consensus are profoundly incompatible with one another, so incompatible that they cannot collectively be taken to support one grand conclusion. That they are understood to have done so might reasonably be taken to suggest that this irresistible conclusion came before, perhaps inspired, the arguments that have been and still are made to support it. I propose that the core assumption that remains unchallenged and unquestioned through all the variations within the diverse traditions of "modern" thought is that the experience and testimony of the individual mind is to be explained away, excluded from consideration when any rational account is made of the nature of human being and of being altogether. In its place we have the grand projects of generalization, solemn efforts to tell our species what we are and what we are not, that were early salients of modern thought. Sociology and anthropology are two examples.

The great new truth into which modernity has delivered us is generally assumed to be that the given world is the creature of accident, that it has climbed Mount Improbable incrementally and over time through a logic of development, refinement, and elaboration internal to itself and sufficient to account exhaustively for all the complexity and variety of which reality and experience are composed. Once it was asserted, and now it is taken to have been proved, that the God of traditional Western religion does not exist, or exists at the remotest margins of time and causality. In either case, an emptiness is thought to have entered human experience with the recognition that an understanding of the physical world can develop and accelerate through disciplines of reasoning for which God is not a given.

It is usual to blame Descartes for the error that has been overcome. This is that same Descartes who proposed the pineal gland as the seat of the soul yet is blamed for creating a dichotomy between the mind/soul and the physical body, a dichotomy that has plagued Western thought, if reports are to be credited. A nonspecialist might wonder how this locating of the soul in the deep interior of the brain differs in principle from locating the moral sense in the prefrontal cortex, as contemporary writers do, to demonstrate how free they are from the errors of Descartes.[14] Descartes is another threshold figure, though he is a marker for notions that have been and must be departed from. It is a given that the march of the modern has many stragglers, indeed that any of us, even the very vanguard, might backslide into Cartesianism in some unguarded moment.

The prestige of the style of thought and argument that

has associated itself with science has had consequences for branches of learning that might seem to have been immune to their influence. A "science of religion," which has been profoundly affected by the imposition of anthropological models of primitivity on this most seminal text, has had enormous consequences for Old Testament scholarship. I am reading a rather strange book titled *How to Read the Bible: A Guide to Scripture, Then and Now,* by James L. Kugel. Kugel's thesis is that the Bible was not in its origins a religious literature and came to be regarded as one only late in the period before the Common Era. Be that as it may. He has this to say about the similarities between the flood narratives in the Epic of Gilgamesh and Genesis: "Someone who reads the Babylonian flood story will likely find it interesting, or perhaps troubling (because of its clear connection to the Genesis account). But any question like 'How are we to apply its lessons to our own lives?' would be greeted by such a reader with incomprehension, or derision. 'Lessons? Why it was written by a bunch of Mesopotamians four thousand years ago!' If that same person then reads what is essentially the same story in the book of Genesis but finds it full of all sorts of uplifting doctrines—well, such a person is either being dishonest or has simply failed to recognize a fundamental fact."[15]

Elegant Babylonia, Greece to Assyria's Rome—ancient,

yes, and far from primitive. There are no grounds for supposing that a "bunch of Mesopotamians" could have had nothing to tell us, or could have said nothing to interest the biblical writers, for that matter. We are entirely in the habit of finding meaning in the writings of ancient India or China or Greece. We are also familiar with the phenomenon of literary allusion. The Sumerian, Babylonian, and Assyrian flood stories are theodicies, certainly among the earliest examples of this interesting genre. Why does catastrophe occur? What does it mean? The nature of the gods and their expectations of and feelings toward human beings are explored in these narratives.

The biblical flood tells the story again, with changes that make it monotheistic, that make the great destruction God's response to human violence and not, as in the Babylonian versions, to the intolerable noise we make. And so on. God is loyal to us, but not because he is dependent on us, as the other gods are dependent on human beings to feed them. In other words, reframing the story is granting its given, that humankind can experience devastation, and then interpreting it in a way that radically restates the conception of God and humankind implied in it. Babylonian culture was powerful and influential. The Gilgamesh epic was found in various forms throughout the ancient Near East. It is absurd to imagine that the most dramatic part of it could simply be patched into the Hebrew Genesis and no one would notice the plagiarism. To retell their story with changes would be to defend against its pagan theological implications, and also to address what are, after all, questions of very great interest.

All this assumes that these ancients had an intellectual life, that they had meaningful awareness of surrounding cultures. Archaeological evidence of continuous contact is well established. Kugel is an Old Testament scholar, certainly better informed than I am about the brilliance of Babylonia. But the implication of the passage quoted above is that the Babylonian origins of the flood narrative exclude it from the kind of reading—for Kugel the discovery of "all sorts of uplifting doctrines"—customarily made of Scripture. The low estimate of Babylonia becomes the basis for a lowered estimate of the Hebrew Bible—the modernist declension. Assuming one narrative is without meaning, we may or must assume the other is, too. This conclusion in all its parts is perfectly arbitrary.

Much of the power of an argument like Kugel's comes from the notion that the information on which it is based is new, another one of those world-transforming thresholds, one of those bold strokes of intellect that burn the fleets of the past. This motif of a shocking newness that must startle us into painful recognition is very much a signature of "the modern," and potent rhetorically, more so because we are conditioned to accept such claims as plausible. But it often achieves its effects by misrepresenting an earlier state of knowledge or simply failing to enquire into it. In 1622, Hugo Grotius, the renowned early legal theorist and scholar, wrote a treatise titled *On the Truth of the Christian Religion.* It was translated into English many times, beginning in the seventeenth century. In sections XVI and XVII Grotius argues for the truth of Genesis on precisely the grounds that other ancient cultures had their own versions of the same stories. These "testimonies of foreigners" show "that the most ancient report was so held among all nations, as the writings of Moses proclaim. For the writings on the 'Origin of the world' which he hath left behind, were, for the most part, the same also in the most ancient histories of the Phoenicians . . . partly, also found among the Indians and Egyptians . . . and the formation of animals, and, lastly, of man, and that, too, according to the Divine Image, is mentioned: and the dominion given to man over the other living creatures: which you may everywhere find in very many writers."[16]

I cannot claim to have found so much similarity as he does between Genesis and ancient literatures in general. My point here is simply that where similarities occur they need not be taken to compromise the authority of the biblical text, even if one cannot agree with Grotius that they can be taken to affirm it. To address Kugel's point more specifically, Grotius is clearly aware of other ancient Near Eastern versions of the story of the Deluge. He says, "Those things which we read of, wrapped up by poets in the licence of fables, the most ancient writers had delivered according to truth, that is, agreeably to Moses, viz.—Berosus, in his history of the Chaldeans; Abydenus, in his of the Assyrians, who even mentions the dove sent forth, as doth also Plutarch, one of the Greeks."[17] Berosus was a Babylonian historian who flourished in the fourth and third centuries before the Common Era. Abydenus was a Greek historian of Assyria who wrote in the third century BCE. Fragments of their work survive in other early texts.

So there were ancient sources available to Grotius in the early seventeenth century which made clear the Babylonians and Assyrians had flood narratives that paralleled the Deluge in Genesis in some detail. Again, that this is a proof of the truth of Moses' account, as Grotius argues it is, that it can in fact be cited in defense of Moses, is clearly open to question. But the notion very common in biblical scholarship since the nineteenth century, reiterated by James Kugel, that the existence of these ancient Mesopotamian narratives was a startling modern discovery which must inevitably raise doubts about the meaningfulness of the scriptural Deluge and about the integrity of Scripture in general is clearly false. The decline of classical learning and the mischaracterization of the nature of traditional belief are both factors in contexts like this one. Another factor that seems to me to be equally important is the great myth and rationale of "the modern," that it places dynamite at the foot of old error and levels its shrines and monuments. Contempt for the past surely accounts for a consistent failure to consult it.

The kind of flawed learnedness required to draw attention to the biblical adaptation of the flood narrative in the Epic of Gilgamesh is a classic instance of what William James called the power of the intellect to shallow.[18] Again, I mention Kugel because I have his book at hand. This kind of scholarship, tending always to the same conclusions, has dominated Old Testament studies from the middle of the nineteenth century. Kugel's very flat statement that someone who takes a different view is "either being dishonest or has simply failed to recognize a fundamental fact" is the kind of claim to the intellectual high ground that is perhaps the most consistent feature of the kind of thought that styles itself modern.

The degree to which debunking is pursued as if it were an urgent crusade, at whatever cost to the wealth of insight into human nature that might come from attending to the record humankind has left, and without regard for the probative standards scholarship as well as science should answer to, may well be the most remarkable feature of the modern period in intellectual history.

# TWO

# The Strange History
# of Altruism

The great breach that separates the modern Western world from its dominant traditions of religion and metaphysics is the prestige of opinion that throws into question the scale of the reality in which the mind participates. Does it open on ultimate truth, at least potentially or in momentary glimpses, or is it an extravagance of nature, brilliantly complex yet created and radically constrained by its biology and by cultural influence? Prior to any statement about the mind is an assumption about the nature of the reality of which it is part, and which is in some degree accessible to it as experience or as knowledge.

Whoever controls the definition of mind controls the definition of humankind itself, and culture, and history. There is something uniquely human in the fact that we can pose questions to ourselves about ourselves, and questions that actually matter, that actually change reality. What we are, what human beings are as individuals and in the categories we assign to them—our assumptions and conclusions on these subjects have had enormous consequences, which were by no means reliably good.

I should declare at the outset my own bias. I believe it is only prudent to make a very high estimate of human nature, first of all in order to contain the worst impulses of human nature, and then to liberate its best impulses. I do not wish to imply malice or calculation on the part of those who insist on a definition of the mind, therefore the human person, which tends to lower us all in our own estimation. It must be obvious, however, that I consider this tendency in modern and contemporary thinking significant and also regrettable.

There is a characteristic certainty that is present structurally in the kind of thought and writing to which I wish to draw attention, a boldness that diminishes its subject. I will refer to this as parascientific literature. By this phrase I mean a robust, and surprisingly conventional, genre of social or political theory or anthropology that makes its case by proceeding, using the science of its moment, from a genesis of human nature in primordial life to a set of general conclusions about what our nature is and must be, together with the ethical, political, economic and/or philosophic implications to be drawn from these conclusions. Its author may or may not be a scientist himself. One of the characterizing traits of this large and burgeoning literature is its confidence that science has given us knowledge sufficient to allow us to answer certain essential questions about the nature of reality, if only by dismissing them. This confidence was already firmly asserted by Auguste Comte, the father of positivism, in 1848. He saw his age prepared for the social regeneration of mankind: "For three centuries men of science have been unconsciously co-operating in the work. They have left no gap of any importance, except in the region of Moral and Social phenomena. And now that man's history has been for the first time systematically considered as a whole, and has been found to be, like all other phenomena, subject to invariable laws, the preparatory labours of modern Science are ended."[1] I seriously doubt that any scientist active today, if pressed, would speak of the sufficiency of our present state of knowledge with equal assurance. Yet in literature of this genre, of which Comte is also an ancestor, that tone of certainty persists, an atavistic trait that defies the evolution of its notional subject.

It is and may always be premature to attempt, let alone

to assert, a closed ontology, to say we know all we need to know in order to assess and define human nature and circumstance. The voices that have said, "There is something more, knowledge to be had beyond and other than this knowledge," have always been right. If there is one great truth contained in the Gilgamesh epic and every other epic venture of human thought, scientific or philosophical or religious, it is that the human mind itself yields the only evidence we can have of the scale of human reality. We have had a place in the universe since it occurred to the first of our species to ask what our place might be. If the answer is that we are an interesting accidental outcome of the workings of physical laws which are themselves accidental, this is as much a statement about ultimate reality as if we were to find that we are indeed a little lower than the angels. To say there is no aspect of being that metaphysics can meaningfully address is a metaphysical statement. To say that metaphysics is a cultural phase or misapprehension that can be put aside is also a metaphysical statement. The notion of accident does nothing to dispel mystery, nothing to diminish scale.

I consider the common account of the sense of emptiness in the modern world to be a faulty diagnosis. If there is in fact an emptiness peculiar to our age it is not because of "the death of God" in the non-Lutheran sense in which that phrase is usually understood. It is not because an ebbing away of faith before the advance of science has impoverished modern experience. Assuming that there is indeed a modern malaise, one contributing factor might be the exclusion of the felt life of the mind from the accounts of reality proposed by the oddly authoritative and deeply influential parascientific literature that has long associated itself with intellectual progress, and the exclusion of felt life from the varieties of thought and art that reflect the influence of these accounts. To some extent even theology has embraced impoverishment, often under the name of secularism, in order to blend more thoroughly into a disheartened cultural landscape. To the great degree that theology has accommodated the parascientific world view, it too has tended to forget the beauty and strangeness of the individual soul, that is, of the world as perceived in the course of a human life, of the mind as it exists in time. But the beauty and strangeness persist just the same. And theology persists, even when it has absorbed as truth theories and interpretations that could reasonably be expected to kill it off. This suggests that its real life is elsewhere, in a place not reached by these doubts and assaults. Subjectivity is the ancient haunt of piety and reverence and long, long thoughts. And the literatures that would dispel such things refuse to acknowledge subjectivity, perhaps because inability has evolved into principle and method.

The advance of science as such need not and should not

preclude acknowledgment of so indubitable a feature of reality as human subjectivity. Quantum physics has raised very radical questions about the legitimacy of the distinction between subjectivity and objectivity. Indeed, there is now a suggestion of the pervasive importance to the deep structures of reality of something of a kind with consciousness. The elusiveness of the mind is a consequence of its centrality, which is both its potency and its limitation. The difficulty with which objectivity can be achieved, to the extent that it ever is achieved, only demonstrates the pervasive importance of subjectivity. I would argue that the absence of mind and subjectivity from parascientific literature is in some part a consequence of the fact that the literature arose and took its form in part as a polemic against religion. And it has persisted, consciously or not, in a strategy for excluding thought of the kind hospitable to religion from the possibility of speaking in its own terms, making its own case. Metaphysics in general has been excluded at the same time, even from philosophy, which since Comte has been associated with this same project of exclusion. The arts have been radically marginalized. In its treatment of human nature the diversity of cultures is left out of account, perhaps to facilitate the making of analogies between our living selves and our hypothetical primitive ancestors, so central to their argument, who can only have been culturally very remote from us indeed.

When history is mentioned, it is usually to point to its follies and errors, which persist to the degree that the light of science has not yet fallen over the whole of human affairs.

There is an odd, undeniable power in this defining of humankind by the exclusion of the things that in fact distinguish us as a species. For this exclusion Comte is not to blame. He famously proposed an elaborate ritualized religion of Humanity, the Grand Being in his parlance. His theory of man and society has no heirs and was in fact shuffled out of positivist thought so promptly and thoroughly that no trace of it can be seen. Comte said that in his new social order, cooperation among people "must be sought in their own inherent tendency to universal love. No calculations of self-interest can rival this social instinct, whether in promptitude and breadth of intuition, or in boldness and tenacity of purpose. True it is that the benevolent emotions have in most cases less intrinsic energy than the selfish. But they have this beautiful quality, that social life not only permits their growth, but stimulates it to an almost unlimited extent, while it holds their antagonists in constant check."[2] To build a grand humanism on the foundation of the sciences was the dream and object of his philosophy.

No theory contemporary with us or influential among us would suggest that humankind is characterized by an "inherent tendency to universal love." Comte wrote in the bloody period of European revolutions and counterrevolutions, and still he believed in the unrivaled power of the "benevolent emotions." Our positivist writers on human nature assume that only self-interest can account for individual behavior. Selfish behavior is assumed to be merely reflexive, though it can be deceptive in its forms, for example when the reward toward which it is directed is social approval. And the deep and persisting acceptance of this vision as indisputable truth has had an epochal significance for the way we think. Comte has had his revenge for the decapitation of his philosophic system in leaving behind a word and concept—altruism, selfless devotion to the good of others—that has deviled parascientific thought ever afterward.

There are inevitable problems with parascientific argument. At best, arguments based on science, no matter what their source, are vulnerable over the medium term, at least, on account of the very commendable tendency of science to change and advance. At this point, the parascientific genre feels like a rear-guard action, a nostalgia for the lost certitudes of positivism. The physical universe, as it is known to us now, is not accessible to the strategies of comprehension that once seemed so exhaustively useful to us. Nevertheless, that it *is* accessible to these strategies is the core faith that continues to animate the writers in the parascientific tradition.

Comte, in the words of the eleventh edition of the *Ency-*

*clopaedia Britannica,* foresaw the evolution of human consciousness beyond its theological and metaphysical stages and into positivism. The article says, "When that stage has been reached, not merely the greater part, but the whole, of our knowledge will be impressed with one character, the character, namely, of positivity or scientificalness, and all our conceptions in every part of knowledge will be thoroughly homogeneous." The impulse to impress all thought with one character is mighty in the literature of parascience, perhaps because it shared its cradle with philosophic monisms like positivism. This is true despite the fact that the traditions of modern thought, however rigorously self-consistent, are not consistent with one another—except in their shared impulse to nullify individual experience, which is perhaps as much a motive as a consequence of their rigor. William James, in an essay on Hegel, says he fears lest that philosopher's monism, "like all religions of the 'one thing needful,' end by sterilizing and occluding the minds of its believers." Perhaps there is something about a sterilized and occluded mind that is strongly associated with missionary zeal, an impatient need to enlist believers, to bring others into the fold. This zeal is another characteristic of the literature I have called parascientific. It has found in the object and glory of Comte's system, altruism, an irresolvable anomaly and an irritant.[3]

If I were a practitioner of the hermeneutics of suspicion, I would note here that, despite their pedagogical tone, these preachments are often intended for those who are in the fold already, meant to reassure them as to the wisdom and actual virtue of their being there. Malthus's *Theory of Population* took its authority from a formula expressing a supposed ratio of the growth of population to the increase of arable land. His contemporaries saw clearly enough what the implications must be for social policy, that the impulse to intervene in the suffering of the poor, an impulse that was under formidable control among them in any case, could, if acted upon, yield only greater suffering among the poor, given the inevitable limits to population size Malthus had seemed to express so objectively. Darwin, famously influenced by Malthus, made the competition for limited resources an elemental, universal principle of life, and, in *The Descent of Man*, folded tribal warfare into the processes of evolution, a notion which meshed nicely with colonialism and with the high esteem in which Europeans of the period held themselves. To proceed from Peter Townsend's observations of overpopulation and starvation among dogs stranded on an island stocked with sheep to the observed fact of starvation among the lower classes in Britain to a formula that makes starvation seem inevitable, as Malthus did—setting aside very practical questions about the distribution of resources, raised by Adam Smith and others—is an instance of parascientific reasoning.

To proceed from biological evidence of our origins among the primates and the primitives to an argument for European supremacy is no less an instance of it. Then there are the writings of Sigmund Freud, by far the greatest and the most interesting contribution to parascientific thought and literature ever made. Freud will be the subject of the next chapter. Recent contributors to the genre include Richard Dawkins and Daniel Dennett, who have given their ideas the effective authority that comes with successful popularization.

However starry-eyed Comte's vision of humanity may have been, there is something in experience that relates, however inexactly, to benevolence and also altruism. There is something in the nature of most of us that takes pleasure in the thought of a humane and benign social order. The tendency of Malthus, and of Darwin in *The Descent of Man*, to counter the humane and also the religious objections to warfare and gross poverty puts compassion or conscience out of play—two of the most potent and engrossing individual experiences, both factors in anyone's sense of right and wrong. This is a suppression of, and an assault on the legitimacy of, an aspect of mind without which the world is indeed impoverished. It is done in the course of proposing an objective, amoral force to which every choice and act is subject. In light of this fact our own sense of things is shown to be delusional, insofar as it might persuade us that our behavior is not essentially self-interested in a narrow sense of that term. By the word "altruism," *altruisme* in French, Comte intended a selfless devotion to the welfare of others which was to fill the place of belief in God left empty by the triumph of scientific positivism. In parascientific literature, the word always appears in a context that questions whether altruism is possible or desirable, or whether apparent instances are real, or what survival benefit might be conferred by it that would account for its undeniable persistence among certain insect colonies.

Herbert Spencer, an important earlier contributor to parascientific literature, is in some degree an exception. In his *Data of Ethics,* published in 1879, he takes up the issue framed by Comte, defending egoism in one chapter and altruism in the next. His argument for egoism is Darwinian: "The law that each creature shall take the benefits and evils of its own nature, be they those derived from ancestry or those due to self-produced modifications, has been the law under which life has evolved thus far; and it must continue to be the law however much farther life may evolve. Whatever qualifications this natural course of action may now or hereafter undergo, are qualifications that cannot, without fatal results, essentially change it. Any arrangements which in a considerable degree prevent superiority from profiting by the rewards of superiority, or shield inferiority from the evils it entails—any arrangements which tend to make it as well to be inferior as to be superior; are arrangements diametrically opposed to the progress of organization and the reaching of a higher life." He goes on to make a case for altruism based on his understanding of reproduction among "the simplest beings," which, he says, "habitually multiply by spontaneous fission." He notes that "though the individuality of the parent infusorium or other protozoon is lost in ceasing to be single, yet the old individual continues to exist in each of the new individuals. When, however, as happens generally with these smallest animals, an interval of quiescence ends in the breaking up of the whole body into minute parts, each of which is the germ of a young one, we see the parent entirely sacrificed in forming progeny."[4]

Spencer is using two modes of scientific thought available to him in the late nineteenth century, Darwinian evolution and the observed division of single-cell animals, to explain the origins of two apparently conflicting ethical impulses or values. Having in a sense legitimized them both by means of these etiologies, he expounds on the ethical, social, and intellectual benefits and difficulties associated with each one, proceeding in the way parascientific argument typically proceeds. Some allusion to the science of the moment is used as the foundation for extrapolations and conclusions that fall far outside the broadest definitions of science. It is to Spencer's credit nevertheless that he acknowledges complexity in this instance. Altruism is a classic problem in the tradition of Darwinist thinking, and Spencer is unusual in granting it reality and a legitimate place in human behavior. It is to be noted, however, that in his considerations of both egoism and altruism, the question might be rephrased in terms of justice or humanity, both of which do from time to time entail some cost to oneself. Justice worth the name tends to exact advantage from anyone who might otherwise enjoy the benefits of relative power. This is a cost which most would be ashamed to notice, and for which they might feel they were fully compensated in the assurance that equity is an active principle. But parascience excludes such subjective considerations.

One might think the insufficiency of any explanatory model to describing essential elements of experience might raise doubts about the model itself, but when the problem of altruism is acknowledged, it is generally addressed by a re-definition of altruism which makes it much more conformable to neo-Darwinist theory. Yet altruism as an idea has not been passive in all this. If I may borrow the language of this genre, it has in some cases parasitized other concepts. By the extremely parsimonious standards of neo-Darwinism, it is the proverbial bad penny, liable to show up anywhere. Michael Gazzaniga reports a question raised by Geoffrey Miller, another evolutionary psychologist. "Most speech appears to transfer useful information from the speaker to the listener, and it costs time and energy. It seems to be altruistic. What fitness benefit can be attained by giving another individual good information? Reviewing the original argument of Richard Dawkins and John Krebs, Miller states, 'Evolution cannot favor altruistic information-sharing any more than it can favor altruistic food-sharing. Therefore, most animals' signals must have evolved to manipulate the behavior of another animal for the signaler's own benefit.' And other animals have evolved to ignore them, because it didn't pay to listen to manipulators." Ergo, it seems, we, alone among the animals, have language. Why the complexity of language and our adeptness in the use of it? Gazzaniga says, "Considering this conundrum, Miller proposes that language's complexities evolved for verbal courtship. This solves the altruism problem by providing a sexual payoff for eloquent speaking by the male and the female." So informative speech is at peril of presenting the theorist with an instance in which a speaker confers benefit to another at cost to himself. But wait! There is manipulation! There is sexual payoff! Does this answer the question about the cost of sharing information? No. Nevertheless, our nature is defined as if determined by the nature of hypothetical primitives, humanlike in their ability to have and give information, but finding neither use nor pleasure in doing so.[5]

This is one instance of the fact that possible altruism can

be detected in many kinds of human behavior, and that where it is even apparently detected it is obviated by elaborations of theory that would have consequences for the understanding of important evolutionary issues—pair bonding, for example, or the early history of the animal brain—since animals supposedly had a capacity for manipulation until it was selected against. Charming as the notion is that our proto-verbal ancestors found mates through eloquent proto-speech—oh, to have been a fly on the wall!—it has very rarely been the case that people have had a pool of eligible others to select among on the basis of some pleasing trait. Endogamy or restricted exogamy among small groups, the bartering of daughters, and status considerations all come into play. It often seems that American anthropologists forget how fluid our culture is and how exceptional our marriage customs are, globally and historically. Pyramus and Thisbe, Eloise and Abelard, Romeo and Juliet, even if they had lived and were able to reproduce, would have been far too exceptional to have influenced the gene pool. And consider those animals who were capable of manipulation and then capable of indifference to it, so that the capacity for it faded away. How did this initial complexity arise? Do animals now have any comparable insight into the motives of others? These neuroscientists tend to say no, though such insight would seem to confer a marked survival advantage. There is more than a little of the just-so story in this theoretical patch on the cost-benefit problem supposedly posed by the phenomenon of human speech. In this way, the specter of altruism, like a lancet fluke in the brain of an ant, distorts Darwinian argument and carries it far beyond the conceptual simplicity for which it is justly famous.

*

I am indebted to Daniel Dennett for the ant and the lancet fluke, a metaphor that comes to mind often as I read in his genre. For example, consider poor Phineas Gage, the railroad worker famous for the accident he suffered and survived more than 150 years ago, an explosion that sent a large iron rod through his skull. Wilson, Pinker, Gazzaniga, and Antonio Damasio all tell this tale to illustrate the point that aspects of behavior we might think of as character or personality are localized in a specific region of the brain, a fact that, by their lights, somehow compromises the idea of individual character and undermines the notion that our amiable traits are intrinsic to our nature.

Very little is really known about Phineas Gage. The lore that surrounds him in parascientific contexts is based on a few anecdotes of uncertain provenance, to the effect that he recovered without significant damage—except to his social skills. Gazzaniga says, "He was reported the next day by the local paper to be pain free." Now, considering that his upper jaw was shattered and he had lost an eye, and that it was 1848, if he was indeed pain free, this should surely suggest damage to the brain. But, together with his rational and coherent speech minutes after the accident, it is taken to suggest instead that somehow his brain escaped injury, except to those parts of the cerebral cortex that had, till then, kept him from being " 'fitful, irreverent, and grossly profane.' " He was twenty-five at the time of the accident. Did he have dependents? Did he have hopes? These questions seem to me of more than novelistic interest in understanding the rage and confusion that emerged in him as he recovered.[6]

How oddly stereotyped this anecdote is through any number of tellings. It is as if there were a Mr. Hyde in us all that would emerge sputtering expletives if our frontal lobes weren't there to restrain him. If any kind of language is human and cultural, it is surely gross profanity, and, after that, irreverence, which must have reverence as a foil to mean anything at all. If to Victorians this behavior seemed like the emergence of the inner savage, this is understandable enough. But from our vantage, the fact that Gage was suddenly disfigured and half blind, that he suffered a prolonged infection of the brain, and that "it took much longer to recover his stamina," according to Gazzaniga, might account for some of the profanity, which, after all, culture and language have prepared for such occasions. But the part of Gage's brain where damage is assumed by modern writers to have been localized is believed to be the seat of the emotions. Therefore —the logic here is unclear to me—his swearing and reviling the heavens could not mean what it means when the rest of us do it. Damasio gives extensive attention to Gage, offering the standard interpretation of the reported change in his character. He cites at some length the case of a "modern Phineas Gage," a patient who, while intellectually undamaged, lost "his ability to choose the most advantageous course of action." Gage himself behaved "dismally" in his compromised ability "to plan for the future, to conduct himself according to the social rules he previously had learned, and to decide on the course of action that ultimately would be most advantageous to his survival." The same could certainly be said as well of Captain Ahab. So perhaps Melville meant to propose that the organ of veneration was located in the leg. My point being that another proper context for the interpretation of Phineas Gage might be others who have suffered gross insult to the body, especially those who have been disfigured by it. And in justice to Gage, the touching fact is that he was employed continually until his final illness. No one considers what might have been the reaction of other people to him when his moving from job to job—his only sin besides cursing and irritability—attracts learned disapprobation.[7]

I trouble the dust of poor Phineas Gage only to make the

point that in these recountings of his afflictions there is no sense at all that he was a human being who thought and felt, a man with a singular and terrible fate. In the absence of an acknowledgment of his subjectivity, his reaction to this disaster is treated as indicating damage to the cerebral machinery, not to his prospects, or his faith, or his self-love. It is as if in telling the tale the writers participate in the absence of compassionate imagination, of benevolence, that they posit for their kind. And there is another point as well. This anecdote is far too important to these statements about the mind, and about human nature. It ought not to be the center of any argument about so important a question as the basis of human nature. It is too remote in time, too phrenological in its initial descriptions, too likely to be contaminated by sensationalism, to have any weight as evidence. Are we really to believe that Gage was not in pain during those thirteen years until his death? How did that terrible exit wound in his skull resolve? No conclusion can be drawn, except that in 1848 a man reacted to severe physical trauma more or less as a man living in 2009 might be expected to do. The stereotyped appearance of this anecdote, the particulars it includes and those whose absence it passes over, and the conclusion that is drawn from it are a perfect demonstration of the difference between parascientific thinking and actual science.

So complete a triumph of one mode of thought as the

neo-Darwinists envision has the look of desolation to some writers in the field, the same desolation that Comte foresaw. He feared that a wholly rational and scientifical understanding would exclude from the world much that is best in it, and much that is essential to a humane understanding of it. As Comte did before him, E. O. Wilson, a well-respected exemplar of this genre, has proposed a new "consilience" that will enrich both science and the arts and humanities by integrating them, a treaty he proposes in the course of asserting a theory of the human mind that is notably unfriendly to his project. He says, "All that has been learned empirically about evolution in general and mental process in particular suggests that the brain is a machine assembled not to understand itself, but to survive. Because these two ends are basically different, the mind unaided by factual knowledge from science sees the world only in little pieces. It throws a spotlight on those portions of the world it must know in order to live to the next day, and surrenders the rest to darkness. For thousands of generations people lived and reproduced with no need to know how the machinery of the brain works. Myth and self-deception, tribal identity and ritual, more than objective truth, gave them the adaptive edge."[8]

When exactly did the mind begin to be aided by "factual knowledge from science"? Where is the evidence that prescientific people see the world "only in little pieces"? Is he speaking of Herodotus? Dante? Michelangelo? Shakespeare? Does knowing "how the machinery of the brain works"— and, in fact, we still do not know how it works—have any implication for the effective use of the mind? Unlike science, the arts and humanities have a deep, strong root in human culture, and have had for millennia. Granting the brilliance of science, there are no grounds for the notion that in its brief history it has transformed human consciousness in the way Wilson describes. The narrowness of Wilson's view of human history seems rather to suggest a parochialism that follows from a belief in science as a kind of magic, as if it existed apart from history and culture, rather than being, in objective truth and inevitably, their product.

\*

For this reason there is in his proposal the implicit assumption that science in its present state is less deeply under unacknowledged cultural influences than it has been historically, as if there were not a history behind his own world view, one that deeply informs his writing. Granting that Wilson's qualifications vastly exceed Spencer's and those of many writers in this genre, the stretch from entomology to human nature is long enough, and his faithfulness to parascientific conventions is close enough, that I feel no hesitation in placing *On Human Nature* and *Consilience* in the same company with *The Data of Ethics* and *The Descent of Man,* rather than with, say, *Discourse on Method* or *The Origin of Species*. The cultural contamination to which science is most vulnerable is the kind that seems to the writer not to be cultural at all, to be instead commonsensical, for instance the very Western, very modern exclusion of subjectivity from the account to be made of human nature.

William James proposed an open epistemology, using the kind of language available to psychology before the positivist purge, appealing to experience, to subjectivity. He said,

> Whoso partakes of a thing enjoys his share, and comes into contact with the thing and its other partakers. But he claims no more. His share in no wise negates the thing or their share; nor does it preclude his possession of reserved and private powers with which they have nothing to do, and which are not all absorbed in the mere function of sharing. Why may not the world be a sort of republican banquet of this sort, where all the qualities of being respect one another's personal sacredness, yet sit at the common table of space and time? . . . Things cohere, but the act of cohesion itself implies but few conditions, and leaves the rest of their qualifications indeterminate. . . . The parts actually known of the universe may comport many ideally possible complements. But as the facts are not the complements, so the knowledge of one is not

the knowledge of the other in anything but the few necessary elements of which all must partake in order to be
together at all.[9]

This is consilient language, too, and aware that it is.
Explicitly religious and political language of a kind that
would be familiar to a nineteenth-century American audience is a weight-bearing element in the architecture of experience he proposes. He says we know anything in the way and
to the degree that we encounter it, and not otherwise. To
claim more is to trench upon a deeper identity that is unknowable by us, a system of contingencies that inheres in the
object of encounter and cannot be excluded from its reality,
and which will not be reached by extrapolation from what
we know about it through our experience. Nor may the
observer himself be absorbed into this universe, as if in accepting definition it must necessarily define him. This is
language that accords uncannily well with the idea of indeterminacy in modern physics, in integrating what we know
about reality with the awareness that unknowability is the
first thing about reality that must be acknowledged. James
published the essay in which it appears in 1882.

\*

In his book *On Human Nature,* published in 1978, E. O.
Wilson does at one point acknowledge the great complexity

of human behavior. He says, "Only techniques beyond our present imagining could hope to achieve even the short-term prediction of the detailed behavior of an individual human being, and such an accomplishment might be beyond the capacity of any conceivable intelligence."[10] Fair enough. These comments on complexity have the smack of actual science about them because they acknowledge the impact of strategies of measurement and of the interests as well as the mere presence of an observer. He is in error when he associates these things with the Heisenberg uncertainty principle, but for one paragraph he does acknowledge the world of scientific awareness we have lived in for the last century.

Still, here is how he interprets a specific kind of behavior he calls "soft-core" altruism, that is, the kind whose benefits redound to the altruist and near kin rather than to his tribe or nation. That he chooses to give this subject a chapter in a book on human nature is itself a cultural choice, one made by Spencer before him, since the possibility of truly selfless behavior has been a point of dispute in this genre since well before Auguste Comte. Wilson says, "Soft-core altruism . . . is ultimately selfish. The 'altruist' expects reciprocation from society for himself or his closest relatives. His good behavior is calculating, often in a wholly conscious way, and his maneuvers are orchestrated by the excruciatingly intricate sanctions and demands of society. The capacity for soft-core altruism can be expected to have evolved primarily by selection of individuals and to be deeply influenced by the vagaries of cultural evolution. Its psychological vehicles are lying, pretense, and deceit, including self-deceit, because the actor is more convincing who believes that his performance is real." Michael Gazzaniga has translated this insight into sophomore-speak: "Everyone (except for me, of course) is a hypocrite. It apparently is just easier to see from the outside than the inside. As we just learned, to pull this off, it helps not to consciously know that you are pulling a fast one, because then you will have less anxiety and thus less chance of getting busted." Steven Pinker takes a different view. There is a book, he says, that "complains that if altruism according to biologists is just helping kin or exchanging favors, both of which serve the interests of one's genes, it would not *really* be altruism after all, but some kind of hypocrisy. This too is a mixup. . . . Genes are a play within a play, not the interior monologue of the players." So for him our conscious motives are entirely distinct from the biological reality that actually prompts behavior. This is a high price to pay for exculpation, in its way the ultimate statement of the modernist impulse to discredit the witness of the mind.[11]

For Wilson, despite his mention of maneuvers and excruciatingly intricate sanctions and vagaries of cultural evolution, complexity is all forgotten. It seems a sociobiologist can bring his perspective to bear on hypothetical actions of a particular kind, without reference to the circumstances in which they might occur, and without what in the circumstances must be called the observer prejudicing the results of his hypothetical observations. No point inquiring of an altruist, should some individual instance of the general phenomenon be found. Should he report other motives than the sociobiologist observed in him, we have already been cautioned against the lying, pretense, deceit, and self-deceit to which his kind—the world over, apparently—are prone. Every seemingly selfless act is really a matter of quid pro quo, whether it occurs in ancient Mesopotamia or modern Japan. We must all know this, since according to Wilson we all use strategies of deception to conceal our true motives from one another. But if we do all know it, how can it be that we expect to deceive one another? What accounts for the impulse to conceal a calculus of fair exchange—the generous act and its socially determined reward—assuming this is what altruism really amounts to?

Herbert Spencer had arrived at the conclusion a century earlier that altruism has its rewards. Yet he concedes the possibility of truly selfless behavior—which, he says, is attended by more than mere reciprocity. "Those [actions] which bring more than equivalents are those not prompted by any thoughts of equivalents. For obviously it is the spontaneous outflow of good nature, not in the larger acts of life only but in all its details, which generates in those around the attachments prompting unstinted benevolence." Spencer's posture is every bit as secular as Wilson's. He is every bit as capable of understanding that altruism brings its returns—public health reforms keep cholera at bay—and yet he can also allow for true generosity. His little portrait of good nature seems almost Dickensian in the context, frank notice of the fact of human community and the pleasures of it, a consideration reliably missing from the sociobiological reckoning of motive and behavior. This may simply be a consequence of his writing more than a century before William Hamilton made his cost-benefit analysis—$r \times b < c$—purporting to show that kinship altruism could be brought under the aegis of self-interest by the understanding that it enhanced the likelihood of survival of one's genes, the formula by which true monism was achieved. Over the years old altruism, the capstone of the Comtean positivist system, had evolved into an insubordinate datum in the grand scheme of rational self-interest, daring to trouble even Darwin himself, who found it among bees. Finally, by means of a mathematical formula, the truth was revealed and the sutures of the system closed.[12]

I find it hard to believe that kinship altruism was where the real mystery lay, however, since the wish to live on in one's descendants is not unusual, even if the words in which it is expressed have lacked imprimatur. Hamilton's formula may have made the generosity of families toward their members comprehensible to the Darwinian mind, but it only sharpens the problem of stranger altruism, which does often appear when a need accessible to help is made known. Most of us have engaged at some time in the imaginative act of identification with the imperiled or suffering. We rehearse it often enough in ballads and novels and films, presumably refining our capacity for self-deception. I should note that later researchers applied game theory to the problem of stranger altruism and worked through the problem to their own satisfaction. They used the "prisoner's dilemma," which, to this poor humanist, seems liable to have prejudiced the outcome, since the given of that game is that each player tries to find a solution least harmful or most beneficial to himself.[13]

Wilson's use of lying, pretense, deceit, and, crucially, self-deceit to explain the reality behind manifest behavior is an important aspect in which Wilson has taken on an inflection of the modern that is not yet apparent in Spencer. A central tenet of the modern world view is that we do not know our own minds, our own motives, our own desires. And—an important corollary—certain well-qualified others *do* know them. I have spoken of the suppression of the testimony of individual consciousness and experience among us, and this is one reason it has fallen silent. We have been persuaded that it is a perjured witness. This is that rare point of convergence among the very diverse schools, Freudianism and behaviorism, for example, that have been called modern, and its consequences have been very great. If I seem to contradict myself, saying in the first place that subjective experience is excluded from this literature and then that it is impugned in it, this contradiction is itself a feature of the genre. Wilson finds in the experience of the altruist "lying, pretense and deceit." Granting that he has said one thing three times—for emphasis, I suppose—he has nevertheless described the intense and calculating interior state of one who ventures a generous act, a state which, since it includes even self-deceit, disqualifies her or him from reporting another set of intentions. What evidence does Wilson offer for the truth of what he says? None at all. He only impugns contrary evidence, the persisting delusion among us that we ourselves do sometimes act from generous motives, and believe that we see others act from them. This is also typical of parascientific argument.

Altruism has been and still is an issue because Darwinist evolutionary theory has considered it to be one. Why would altruism persist as a trait, when evolution would necessarily select against the conferring of benefit to another at cost to oneself? Hamilton's rule is thought to have resolved the issue by the power of cost-benefit analysis. A scenario involving the rescue of a drowning child demonstrates, mathematically, without the slightest reference to anything that has happened or might happen in the real world, that a parent would be likely to rescue a child of his own, since that child is presumably the bearer of half his parent's genetic inheritance —possibly including the genetic predisposition to altruism. To quote Lee Alan Dugatkin, "If grandchildren are in need of rescue, the net benefit received by the altruist is cut in half," and so on as the degree of consanguinity diminishes.[14] Note the impossibly narrow set of factors in play here. The potential cost ($c$) is not the value—even genetic value—invested in the child by the rescuer and potentially lost by him but only the risk to the rescuer's own physical well-being. Nor is the potential benefit ($b$) the emotional one of recovering the child, or even of feeling adequate to a critical situation, but only of enhancing the likelihood that a gene will survive into another generation.

All this is plausible if the experience and testimony of humankind is not to be credited, if reflection and emotion are only the means by which the genes that have colonized us manipulate us for their purposes. How are "we" to be located in all this? What are "we" if we must be bribed and seduced by illusory sensations we call love or courage or benevolence? Why need our genes conjure these better angels, when, presumably, the species of toads and butterflies whose ways are said to demonstrate the power of Hamilton's rule flourish without them? What are "we" if our hopes of ourselves are higher than, or contrary to, the reality by which we are in fact governed? If these feelings are so strong for us that our true motives awaited the coming of sociobiology in order to be revealed to us, might not the hope of these illusory rewards have begun at some point to function as our true motive, one that would tend to express itself (given the nature of the deception) in ways that were altruistic in the ordinary sense of the word? And, assuming that termites are without illusion, does this possibility not create a problem for Hamilton's rule, insofar as it is taken to be a description of both termite and human behavior? If these ingratiating deceits and delusions were called by kinder names, they might seem to argue for the kind of thing theology calls ensoulment. The so-called illusions, delusions, deceptions, and self-deceptions about which parascience as a project is so inclined to fret make up a great part of the margin between ourselves and the other creatures that we call our humanity. And, I will argue, they are the implicit subject of that project. So, clearly, they have an important reality. They are, whatever else, the workings of our species' remarkable brain. To exclude them from consideration in an account of human nature makes no sense at all.

The Hamilton equation describes a circumstance that is entirely theoretical, and inevitably so. Instances of this ideal test, the drowning child imagined by J. B. S. Haldane, no less, the child who is to be rescued or not by kin or strangers, would be far too rare among possibly altruistic events to support generalization. Do elderly mothers go unrescued, being past their childbearing years? Do firefighters run into burning houses looking for kith and kin? In how many instances would those disposed to altruism die in the rescue of strangers whose genetic proclivities were entirely unknown to them? Then how likely would it be that a gene for altruism would persist in a population, given Hamilton's account of it? Whether the formula can be applied to bees and termites and naked mole rats is a judgment that can be left only to specialists, though the observer effect must be assumed to be in play among specialists, too. And a reader in this literature has no more chance of testing the validity of their observations than she has of splitting a photon.

We have been told to disallow the intense and emotional subjective considerations a human altruist is likely to ponder, and to do so in deference to a mathematical formula that can never be made subject to any test in a human population. It is consistent with the genre of parascience, however, that this formula is applied with great confidence to the nature of our species. Hamilton himself said he "realized from common experience that university people sometimes don't react well to common sense, and in any case most of them listened to it harder if you first intimidate them with equations."[15] If one may judge from the impact of his equation on his field, this is certainly true. Hamilton's rule is really the transmogrification of a statement Thomas Huxley had made a century before him. If his formula is taken seriously, it precludes any other conclusion than that altruism, where it occurs at all, occurs within families, on account of the "selfishness" of a gene. That is, it occurs only in circumstances that reduce as far as possible the degree to which the behavior can be called altruistic, not in order to refine the definition of the word but in order to make the phenomenon seem assimilable to a theory.

Spencer's mention of the "parent infusorium," Freud's mention of "the stores of libido by means of which the cells of the soma are attached to one another," for that matter Auguste Comte's pondering the physiology of the brain—such things have lent authority to philosophies that in turn deeply influence the thought of subsequent generations.[16] And by dint of sheer historical importance they have legitimized a style of argument—the use of fragments of what in the writer's moment is taken to be scientific truth—to leverage the broadest statements on the largest subjects.

Thinkers like Richard Dawkins and Daniel Dennett attribute the universe in all its complexity to accident. In this view, accident defines over time the range of the possible because circumstances develop which create an effect of optimization, an enhanced suitability of life forms for survival, individual and genetic, in whatever conditions pertain. Not surprisingly, Dennett likens this process to an algorithm. The inevitable iterations of variation on one hand and selection on the other have yielded all that exists or has ever existed. The human mind is one more, very splendid, product of these iterations. Of course Dennett assumes that the human mind was and is profoundly wrong about its origins and nature. This can be true despite the unsentimental workings of natural selection because a new layer has been superadded to reality by Dennett, Dawkins, and others to allow for the anomalous character of the brain/mind. This entity or phenomenon is called the meme, by analogy to the gene. It is a selfish, brain-colonizing personal or cultural concept, idea, or memory that survives by proliferating, implanting itself in other brains. Dawkins says, "Examples of memes are tunes, ideas, catch-phrases, clothes fashions, ways of making pots or building arches. Just as genes propagate themselves in the gene pool by leaping from body to body via sperms or eggs, so memes propagate themselves in the meme pool by leaping from brain to brain via a process which, in the broad sense, can be called imitation." He quotes his colleague N. K. Humphrey: "Memes should be regarded as living structures, not just metaphorically but technically. When you plant a fertile meme in my mind, you literally parasitize my brain, turning it into a vehicle for the meme's propagation in just the way that a virus may parasitize the genetic mechanism of a host cell. And this isn't just a way of talking —the meme for, say, 'belief in life after death' is actually realized physically, millions of times over, as a structure in the nervous systems of individual men the world over."[17]

The meme is not a notion I can dismiss out of hand. It seems to me to describe as well as anything does the obdurate persistence and influence of the genre of writing I have called parascientific. This piece of evidence for its reality might not please its originators, who always seem to assume their own immunity from the illusions and distractions that plague the rest of us. Still, aware as I am that Einstein's cosmological constant was first of all a sort of fudge, in his view a blunder, I am willing to concede that this idea cannot be wholly discredited by its obvious usefulness to those who have proposed it. It does raise questions within the terms of their conceptual universe, however. For example, let us say altruism is a meme, inexplicably persistent, as other traits associated with religion are also. Then is there any need to make a genetic or sociobiological account of it? If its purpose is to have a part in sustaining related memes by which it would also be sustained, such as "family" or "religious community," would it be dependent on the process of Darwinian selection represented in the theoretical rescue/non-rescue of the drowning child?

To put the question in more general terms: the role of the meme in this school of thought is to account for the human mind and the promiscuous melange of truth and error, science and mythology, that abides in it and governs it, sometimes promoting and sometimes thwarting the best interests of the organism and the species. Then why assume a genetic basis for any human behavior? Memes would appear to have sprung free from direct dependency on our genes, and to be able to do so potentially where they have not yet done so in fact. And assuming that Homo sapiens are unique in this experience of meme colonization, does this theory not set apart something that might be called human nature, that is, certain qualities of humankind that are unique to us, and not to be accounted for by analogies between ourselves and the hymenoptera? Sociobiology, with its dependency on gradualist neo-Darwinism, is difficult to reconcile with these incorporeal, free-floating, highly contagious memes which, in theory, have somehow managed to grow our physical brains to accommodate their own survival and propagation. Only consider the physiological and societal consequences of those big heads of ours in terms of maternal and infant mortality, the helplessness of infants, and the importance to us of culture, among other things. Does not this theory implicitly marginalize gene-based accounts of human behavior?

Memes and Hamiltonian genes do resemble each other, though only as a stone resembles an oyster. They differ in that the first has a status that is something less than hypothetical, while, of course, genes are actual and are thoroughly mapped and studied. The traits of this notional meme align nicely with the Hamiltonian idea of "selfishness," that is, the idea that, like the gene, the meme impacts the organism's function and behavior to perpetuate its own existence through generations. Granting that such an entity as a meme would have an interest in the survival of the one species that can serve as the vehicle of its spread and perpetuation, in individual cases this is clearly at odds with the personal survival of human beings. To choose an illustration of the point at random—the Horst Wessel Lied, a song written in celebration of fallen comrades by a young man who was himself assassinated, was, so to speak, an important modern carrier of that ancient meme and killer of young men, *dulce et decorum est pro patria mori*. I think it is generally believed that the martyrdoms of early Christians did much to anchor their religion in the culture of the Mediterranean world. The best case to be made for the correctness of the notion that there are indeed memes, and that they do indeed perpetuate themselves in human culture over time, would be the potency they acquire in the very fact of the destruction of the young and strong. When factions or nations turn on each other, those who win lose from the point of view of the species, in destroying the genetic wealth of their adversaries, and no "selfishness," however leveraged by equations, intervenes to limit the losses we as a species suffer.

My point is that, despite a superficial resemblance between the hypothetical meme and the hypothetically "selfish" gene, owed no doubt to their shared intellectual paternity, each theory obviates the other, or at best creates any number of disputed boundaries between them. This would be interesting and nothing more than interesting if the neo-Darwinism of Hamilton, Dawkins, Dennett, and others did not offer itself as a monism, as the one thing needful, the one sufficient account for literally everything. If altruism has seemed to be the ragged edge of Darwinism, a worry to T. H. Huxley, finally tucked out of sight by Hamilton's formula, why should they be so unperturbed by the fact that these mighty memes, granting their existence here for the purposes of argument, provide an alternative account for the whole of human behavior? Why war? *Dulce et decorum est.* Why altruism? It is more blessed to give than to receive. Whence the bonds of family? I love all the dear silver that shines in her hair, and the brow that is wrinkled and furrowed with care.

Ah, but what is the origin of these memes? Once a shaman was right about where game was to be found, and religion was up and running. But a good many human behaviors and cultural patterns run counter to religion or have no clear source in it. In any case, a stickler might wonder whether some crude metaphysics would not have lurked behind the role of shaman and the idea of consulting him, if shamanism itself ought not to be called a meme. For that matter, one might wonder if some unacknowledged metaphysics lurks behind the parascientific positing of these immortal, incorporeal destinies that possess us to their own inscrutable ends, rather in the manner of the gods of Greek mythology. The question of origins bears a certain similarity to the questions raised by E. O. Wilson's remarks on altruism. What is the nature of the reality we inhabit if we have to conceal self-interested motives? If nature runs on self-interest to its own ultimate enhancement and ours, where is the shame in it? Isn't shame as extraneous to the workings of the world, understood from a Hamiltonian perspective, as generosity itself would be? We might be tempted to patch in a meme here—I was hungry and you fed me, I was naked and you clothed me—but if we did, then we would have proposed a sufficient account of altruism, making Hamilton's equation entirely unnecessary. And, since the benefactor would have been acting purely at the behest of the meme, we would also have excluded deception and self-deception as factors in the altruistic act.

The neo-Darwinism of Hamilton and others shares one consequence with meme theory: both of them represent the mind as a passive conduit of other purposes than those the mind ascribes to itself. It reiterates that essential modernist position, that our minds are not our own. The conviction so generally shared among us, that we think in some ordinary sense of that word, that we reason and learn and choose as individuals in response to our circumstances and capacities, is simply—the one, crucial point of agreement between these otherwise incompatible theories—a persisting illusion serving a force or a process that is essentially unknown and indifferent to us.

*

The comparison that is salient here is between the accidental and the intentional in terms of their consequences for the interpretation of anything. In the course of my reading, I have come to the conclusion that the random, the accidental, have a strong attraction for many writers because they simplify by delimiting. Why is there something rather than nothing? Accident. Accident narrows the range of appropriate strategies of interpretation, while intention very much broadens it. Accident closes on itself, while intention implies that, in and beyond any particular fact or circumstance, there is vastly more to be understood. Intention is implicitly communicative, because an actor is described in any intentional act. Why is the human brain the most complex object known to exist in the universe? Because the elaborations of the mammalian brain that promoted the survival of the organism overshot the mark in our case. Or because it is intrinsic to our role in the universe as thinkers and perceivers, participants in a singular capacity for wonder as well as for comprehension.

The anomalies that plague accident as an explanatory model—the human mind, most notably—are no problem at all if it is assumed that accident does not explain us, that we are meant to be human, that is, to be aware and capable in the ways the mind—and how else to describe the mind?— makes us aware and capable. And what are those ways? Every poem, theory, philanthropy, invention, scandal, hoax, and crime of violence tells us more. No aspect of reality, from this point of view, need be simplified or limited to fit an explanatory model. One would think that the inadequacy of any model to deal with the complexity of its subject would make its proponents a bit tentative, but in fact the tendency of the kind of thought I wish to draw attention to is to deny the reality of phenomena it cannot accommodate, or to scold them for their irksome, atavistic persistence.

This is surely an odd way to proceed, especially in light

of the fact that these schools of thought regard themselves as scientific, or as accepting of certain scientific insights that must lead any honest and enlightened person to embrace their view of things. The Berkeley philosopher John Searle objects to the commonly held conception that "suggests that science names a specific kind of ontology, as if there were a scientific reality that is different from, for example, the reality of common sense." He says, "I think that is profoundly mistaken." And he says, "There is no such thing as the scientific world. There is, rather, just the world, and what we are trying to do is describe how it works and describe our situation in it."[18] This seems to me so true that I would consider the statement obvious, or, as the philosophers say, trivial, if it did not make a claim, necessary in the circumstances, for the relevance to the study of mind of the fullness of mental experience.

John Searle is no transcendentalist. I do not wish to seem to recruit him in support of the religious position I have just declared. I do, however, take comfort in the fact that his objections to contemporary philosophic thinking about consciousness and mental phenomena are very like mine. He says of certain arguments offered by philosophers of the materialist school, "What they suggest is that these people are determined to try to show that our ordinary common-sense notions of the mental do not name anything in the real world, and they are willing to advance any argument that they can think of for this conclusion."[19] This is not a new state of affairs, nor one limited to Searle's colleagues or to writers in fields related to his. The subject that interests me is in fact the persistence, through the very long period we still call "modern" and into the present, of something like a polemic against the mind—not mind as misnomer, nor as the construct of an untenable dualism, but mind in more or less the fullest sense of the word.

The resourcefulness Searle speaks of, the recourse to "any argument they can think of," seems to me sometimes to be the unifying principle behind an apparent diversity of important schools and theories. Anthropology, positivism, Nietzscheanism in its various forms, Freudian and behaviorist psychology have all brought their insights to bear on this subject.

The word "modern" is itself a problem, since it implies a Promethean rescue from whatever it was that went before, a rupture so complete as to make context irrelevant. Yet if one were to imagine a row of schoolroom modernists hanging beside the schoolroom poets, Marx, Nietzsche, and Wellhausen beside Bryant, Longfellow, and Whittier, one would notice a marked similarity among them of pince-nez and cravat. The modern has been modern for a very long time. As a consequence of its iconic status, the contemporary remains very much in its shadow. Little that is contemporary is not also modern, and little that is modern departs as cleanly from its precursors as myth would have us believe. In one important particular, however, there seems to have been an authentic modern schism whose consequences are persistent and profound. Our conception of the significance of humankind in and for the universe has shrunk to the point that the very idea we ever imagined we might be significant on this scale now seems preposterous. These assumptions about what we are and are not preclude not only religion but also the whole enterprise of metaphysical thought. That the debate about the nature of the mind has tended to center on religion is a distraction which has nevertheless exerted a profound influence on the more central issue. While it may not have been true necessarily, it has been true in fact that the renunciation of religion in the name of reason and progress has been strongly associated with a curtailment of the assumed capacities of the mind.

# THREE

# The Freudian Self

Toward the end of his life, Carl Jung, remembering his association and his differences with Sigmund Freud, says, "Above all, Freud's attitude toward the spirit seemed to me highly questionable. Wherever, in a person or in a work of art, an expression of spirituality (in the intellectual, not the supernatural sense) came to light, he suspected it, and insinuated that it was repressed sexuality. Anything that could not be directly interpreted as sexuality he referred to as 'psychosexuality.' I protested that this hypothesis, carried to its logical conclusion, would lead to an annihilating judgment upon culture. Culture would then appear as a mere farce, the morbid consequence of repressed sexuality. 'Yes,' he assented, 'so it is, and that is just a curse of fate against which we are powerless to contend.' "[1]

In the context of the time, Freud's aversion to what is here called "spirituality" is wholly understandable. He asked Jung "never to abandon the sexual theory," telling him, "You see, we must make a dogma of it, an unshakeable bulwark." When Jung asked, "A bulwark—against what?" Freud replied, "Against the black tide of mud . . . of occultism."[2] Though Jung does not share my interpretation of Freud's meaning, which he finds mysterious, I would suggest that these words support an interpretation of the intention behind his metapsychological writing as a whole, which rests so heavily on this theory. Jung reports another conversation with Freud about "precognition and parapsychology in general," which Freud rejected as nonsense. Jung says,

> While Freud was going on in this way, I had a curious sensation. It was as if my diaphragm were made of iron and were becoming red-hot—a glowing vault. And at that moment there was such a loud report in the bookcase . . . that we both started up in alarm, fearing the thing was going to topple over on us. I said to Freud: "There, that is an example of a so-called catalytic exteriorization phenomenon."
>
> "Oh, come,' he exclaimed. 'That is sheer bosh.' "[3]

That Freud could have placed hopes in a disciple capable of belief in this sort of thing—Jung says, "The question of the chthonic spirit has occupied me ever since I began to delve into the world of alchemy"—is surely remarkable. Though Freud is gracious and conciliatory toward the younger man in letters to him that refer to this episode, and to occultism itself, from Freud's side the relationship must have been extremely tense. Jung reports another conversation in which his consuming interest in bog corpses actually caused Freud to faint. "Afterward he said to me that he was convinced that all this chatter about corpses meant I had death wishes toward him." And, according to Jung, he fainted again when he heard the theory of the primal father disputed.[4]

The tightly self-referential character of what Freud calls sexuality excludes the chthonic, the folkloric, the mystical, all very familiar conceptual terms of the "intellectual spirituality" abroad in that place and time, and which had begun to emerge in Jung's thought for all the world as if he were discovering them for himself. Early twentieth-century Europe could only have impressed itself very deeply on Freud's understanding of civilization, religion, and human nature. Grand theories with pointed reference to persons like himself were very much in the air, in the streets and the press and the lecture halls, of early twentieth-century Vienna. As the son of Jews who had immigrated into Vienna from the Czech region of the old Austro-Hungarian Empire, he could hardly have been unaware of the violent hostility toward Jews and Czechs excited by the racial nationalism of the pan-Germanist movements in the capital. Nor could his Jewish patients have been unaware of it. In 1899 Karl Lueger, the mayor of Vienna, made a speech in which he spoke of "Jews exercising a 'terrorism worse than which cannot be imagined,'" of the need for "'liberating the Christian people from the domination of Jewry.'" And again he called Jews "'these beasts of prey in human form,'" and so on.[5] It seems he was only galvanizing his base, as we say, and pursued no anti-Semitic policies. Such was the atmosphere of the city where Freud was beginning his career, and where the young Adolf Hitler was struggling to establish himself as a painter. It has been a convention of history to treat Austria as having been on the peripheries of catastrophe, as having been swept up in events visited on central Europe by Hitler, despite the fact that Hitler was himself an Austrian who developed his political views in Vienna. At the beginning of the twentieth century, and of his career as a writer on the nature of the human psyche, Freud would have seen the emergence in Vienna of anti-Semitism in its virulent modern form. Yet interpreters of Freud seem to treat his theories as if they have no significant historical context except that provided by Copernicus and Darwin, as if they formed in a weatherless vacuum of some kind, in the pure light of perspicuous intellect.

Freud himself encourages this view of his metapsychological theories, proceeding as he does at the highest possible level of generalization, a level paradoxically sustained both despite and by means of the omission of that sizable portion of the human race who do not live on the European continent. This is not meant as criticism. Instead, I wish to draw attention to the intensity as well as the implications of his insistence, despite this, on a universal human character with a single narrative shaping individual and collective life. To put the matter in very few words, I will suggest that, in a Europe fascinated by notions of the radical importance of racial, cultural, and national difference, Freud is creating another, opposing anthropology, one that excludes these categories altogether. That is to say, whatever problems attend the reduction of human experience to a suite of responses to a supposed primal event, altogether unspecified in place and time—the parricide and feast of the primal horde—this narrative, without sentiment or optimism, erases difference and universalizes the anxiety and discontent attested to on every side in Europe as the inevitable phylogenetic circumstance of civilized human beings, rather than particularizing it as an effect of historical circumstance.

There were highly influential accounts of the origins of an assumed anomie variously asserted by Fichte, Maurras, Spengler, and others, an inauthenticity plaguing the European mind that had its roots in the presence of foreign elements in blood, language, and culture. And there was Freud, granting the reality of these discomforts and asserting their origins in the nature of the mind itself. When, in *The Future of an Illusion,* he says, "I scorn to distinguish between culture and civilization," he is explicitly rejecting a distinction that had been current in Europe since Fichte, that contrasted the shallow cosmopolitanism of civilization, with its mingling of populations, with the supposed profundity of pure and autochthonous culture. In *The Decline of the West,* published in 1918, Oswald Spengler wrote, "*Culture and Civilization*—the living body of a soul and the mummy of it. For Western existence the distinction lies at about the year 1800—on the one side of that frontier life in fullness and sureness of itself, formed by growth from within, in one great uninterrupted evolution from Gothic childhood to Goethe and Napoleon, and on the other the autumnal, artificial, rootless life of our great cities, under forms fashioned by the intellect." Freud himself would have been seen as cosmopolitan in this negative sense, as would many of his patients.[6]

Jews in Vienna at that time had every reason to be anxious, even "neurotic," given the surge of anti-Semitism in the

Dreyfus affair and the notorious blood libel trial in Russia, not to mention the early and, for them, recent electoral success of an anti-Semitic party in Vienna. Nothing in European history could encourage confidence that this ancient antagonism would find any rational bounds. There had been liberalizing trends, emancipations, political accommodations that permitted Jews to assimilate and flourish, and to contribute very richly to the brilliance of the civilization. And their contributions could be turned against them, as the corruption of culture rather than its enrichment, as the attenuation of the deeper bond of blood and soil that, so the story went, had once rooted human life in nature and meaning, in authenticity. The intellectual prestige of this world view may be hard to credit now, but it was great and lasting, and would have been a presence in the thoughts of cultured Jews, as much a presence to them as were the street bullies whose resentments it dignified.

If Freud's interpretation of neurosis and anxiety in his patients might appear to be itself repression or sublimation, a robust denial of the fact that he and they had more than ample reason for unease, his metapsychological essays address this hostile world view implicitly but quite directly, opposing it at every major point by means of a counternarrative, a radically different psychology and anthropology. Parapsychology had its vogue, as Jung's anecdote illustrates, and Freud wrote an essay explaining it away as, in effect, a trick of the mind. Gustave Le Bon published his book on the nature of crowds, ascribing the special character of mass behavior to a racial unconscious, and Freud responded that the special character of the crowd was libido, eros, mutual love. Europe was obsessed with myths of origins, and Freud wrote *Totem and Taboo*, proposing a single, universal myth to explain the etiology of human nature and culture. Europe was obsessed with its discontents, and Freud acknowledged the discomforts, which are also the price, of civilization and its benefits. The distinctive self-enclosed yet universal Freudian persona was an implicit challenge to a conception of the character of the unconscious as a substratum of racial and national identity. Rereading Freud, I have come to the conclusion that his essays, and therefore very central features of his thought, most notably the murder of the primal father with all its consequences, were meant to confute theories of race and nation that were becoming increasingly predominant as he wrote. This is not to say that he was not persuaded of their truth, only that his deep concern that they be maintained as a bulwark against "black mud," that they should have seemed to Jung to have had something like a religious significance for him, is entirely understandable.

Adding to the emotional complexity of the Jews' situation in Vienna was the fact that they loved the brilliant city, distinguished themselves in its literary life and in its university faculties, and clung, no doubt, to the assurances they could find in the very fact that so much of Viennese life was now open to them. In *The Interpretation of Dreams,* published in 1900, Freud mentions that his being appointed to a professorship had seemed unlikely to him because of "denominational considerations," and he repeats the story of an insult to his father, which his father described to him so he would know how much worse things had been in the past. He describes a schoolboy identification with Semitic Hannibal which grew from the fact of being made aware by the other students of his own membership in an "alien race." Yet, with whatever degree of bitterness and irony, he folds the phenomenon of anti-Semitism into his understanding of human nature and society. In *Civilization and Its Discontents* he says, "It is clearly not easy for men to give up the satisfaction of this inclination to aggression. They do not feel comfortable without it. The advantage which a comparatively small cultural group offers of allowing this instinct an outlet in the form of hostility against intruders is not to be despised. It is always possible to bind together a considerable number of people in love, so long as there are other people left over to receive the manifestations of their aggressiveness." He continues, "Neither was it an unaccountable chance that the dream of a Germanic world-dominion called for anti-semitism as its complement; and it is intelligible that the attempt to establish a new, communist civilization in Russia should find its psychological support in the persecution of the bourgeois. One only wonders, with concern, what the Soviets will do after they have wiped out their bourgeois."[7]

It is painful to see Freud, in 1930, putting that Germanic dream in the past tense and focussing his concern only on Russia. When Freud finally vents his grief at the disastrous turn Europe had taken after the Versailles Treaty, he does so in a contemptuous book-length "psychological study" of Thomas Woodrow Wilson, making no mention of Adolf Hitler, who was surely a more interesting subject for analysis, or of the European context that anticipated and prepared the way for his ascent to power.

In his study of Wilson, Freud quotes the account by the president's secretary, Joseph Tumulty, of a scene in the cabinet meeting room after Wilson had asked Congress to approve a declaration of war against Germany. "For a while he sat silent and pale in the Cabinet Room. At last he said: 'Think what it was they were applauding. My message today was a message of death for our young men. How strange it seems to applaud that.' Then Wilson reads a sympathetic letter from someone he called a 'fine old man.' Then, 'as he said this, the President drew his handkerchief from his pocket, wiped away great tears that stood in his eyes, and then laying his head on the Cabinet table sobbed as if he had been a child." True or not, Freud found great significance in this anecdote. His interpretation of the moment is very like a taunt—"Little Tommy Wilson still needed enormously the tender sympathy and approval of his 'incomparable father.'" Elsewhere Freud says of the president's boyhood, "A more masculine boy than Tommy Wilson would have felt hostility to the *mores* of the family and community in which the Minister's son was reared; but he felt no impulse to revolt. His masculinity was feeble. His Ego-Ideal was not hostile to the ideals of his family or his community. The problems of his life arose not from conflicts with his environment but from conflicts within his own nature. He would have had to face those conflicts if he had been brought up in the comparative freedom of European civilization. The screen of rationalizations which allowed him to live all his life without facing his passivity to his father would have fallen early on the continent of Europe."[8]

The manuscript of this "study" was completed in 1932, not long before the Nazis demonstrated their power at the polls and Hitler became chancellor of Germany. Still, Freud can represent European civilization as intrinsically healthier than Lollard America, psychologically speaking. To address personality this way, as formed by a specific culture, is a departure for Freud. One would never know from his work as a whole that the combined effects of Wyclif, Calvin, and Wesley could be sufficient to interfere in the Oedipal drama. For the president to have wept after requesting a declaration of war hardly seems symptomatic of instability or of "feeble masculinity," nor is Freud's case strengthened by the discovery, through the methods of his science, that Wilson wanted to be his father's wife. This odd piece of work is worth notice only as a demonstration of Freud's deep loyalty to European civilization, expressed directly and indirectly as well in his displaced rage at Woodrow Wilson.

The posture, the language, and the extraordinary mythopoesis Freud sustains in his metapsychological essays are sui generis in a degree that comes near making them immune to criticism from a scientific perspective, though Freud does claim for them the authority of science. If they are intended, as I believe they are, to counter a dominant strain of thought, one that incorporated philosophy, psychology, anthropology, biology, and linguistics to produce and confirm an ideology of racial nationalism, then Freud can be seen as offering another framework of understanding that excludes race and nation as essential elements of human nature. The scale of his project and his choices of subject and emphasis are consistent with this interpretation of his essays, which are not by any means an inevitable outgrowth of his analyses of individual patients.

The importance Freud attaches to the Oedipal crime, his insistence on the reality of this event and its consequences, seems incomprehensible as a discovery of psychoanalytic research but entirely comprehensible if it is understood as a strategy for creating a model of human nature that enters history already moral and religious—in the negative or at least deeply ambivalent sense in which Freud uses those terms—and already guilty and self-alienated. If this model is accepted, then morals can have had no genealogy. There can have been no historical moment in which, as Nietzsche claims, the nobility of Europe was undermined by a Jewish slave religion. Nietzsche says, "It has been the Jews who have, with terrifying consistency, dared to undertake the reversal of the aristocratic value equation (good = noble = powerful = beautiful = happy = blessed) and have held on to it tenaciously by the teeth of the most unfathomable hatred (the hatred of the powerless)."[9] I have been rebuked so often by his academic admirers for finding evidence of anti-Semitism in passages like this one that I will not raise the issue here. My point is simply that Nietzsche sees morality as arising out of cultural history, modern morality from the influence on European values of the Jews, by way of Christianity. For Freud, there is no imagination of a state of things before that first parricide, and only an elaboration of its consequences after it. There were no pre-existing values to have been transvalued, and there has been no possibility of a rupture in the persistence of the moral and psychological consequences it entailed.

Freud is of one mind in a number of important particulars with the strain of thought dominant in his place and time. Spengler said, "Civilization is nothing but tension."[10] Freud agrees that civilization is not a happy condition for human beings, and that human beings contain primordial selves from whom they are alienated by the demands of civilized life. He agrees with Nietzsche that religion is a constraining illusion, the basis of an archaic morality unworthy of the deference paid to it. He takes Darwinism to have disposed of the old prejudice that set humankind apart from the animals. The narratives of loss, violation, contagion, and so on that are characteristic of the period are narratives of victimization, and Freud assumes an extraordinarily passive self, acted upon and deeply threatened by external influences, past and present. His model of the self, made passive by constraints imposed on it through the internalization of an identity not its own, one that is indeed antagonistic and intimidating, is broadly consistent with versions of the self that flourished among his contemporaries.

Freud departs from the prevailing narrative in that he finds the discomforts of civilization both inevitable and preferable to a state in which its constraints did not exist. Civilization is not, for him, visited on the self by other people or created in the course of a collective history of acculturation and interaction. It is generated, in its essential elements, from a primal act, the murder and ingesting of the father, which persists phylogenetically in every individual and all generations, as conscience, as religion, in repression and sublimation. Granting the discomforts, no one is to blame for them. They are not the consequence of decline, since their origin lies in an event that took place at the beginning of human time. They are not the consequence of deracination, since the Freudian self is at ease nowhere and has no kindred beyond father and mother, who offer identity in a somewhat negative sense, standing in place of the principals in that ancient, Oedipal crime.

Religion is a single, universal consequence of that same cannibal feast, out of which arose the god who terrifies and protects like the Freudian father and whose authority is preserved in the guilt that persists in human experience though its source, the memory behind it, is repressed. In other words, since it lies at the root of the emergence of the human psyche, once in the primal act itself and again in every (male) infant, religion profoundly marks every individual and society in an essentially similar way. Therefore it cannot be the conflict of religious cultures that accounts for unease. Instead, from the beginning unease is implanted in experience together with religion, with which it is more or less identical. The argument in *Moses and Monotheism* that the ancient Hebrews murdered Moses and then, so to speak, resurrected him, repressing the memory of the crime and preserving and magnifying his authority, conforms Judaism to the universal, psychologically driven pattern also to be seen in the death and resurrection of Christ.

Related to all this is the problem, a corollary of Darwinism, of accounting for the power of a morality that runs counter to self-interest, and therefore counter to the evolutionary interests of the species, insofar as they would be served by the relentless assertion of advantage on the part of the strong. It has rarely seemed agreeable or even practical to conform human behavior wholly to, in Herbert Spencer's words, "the law that each creature shall take the benefits and the evils of its own nature." This, he says, "has been the law under which life has evolved thus far; and it must continue to be the law however much further life may evolve."[11] Yet if it is indeed a law of nature, it is departed from a good deal more frequently than, say, the law of gravity, or the second law of thermodynamics.

That we are seemingly free to behave altruistically, at least to the degree that it is altruistic not to press every advantage, and are able to sustain value systems that encourage generosity or selflessness, is an anomaly that has troubled

Darwinist thinking since T. H. Huxley. Freud solves the riddle of moral behavior, obedience to restraint and obligation, by placing its source in that primordial crime. When Freud derived his "primal horde" from Darwin, he put the notion of it to uses that depart from Darwinist orthodoxy in making its overwhelming impact on subsequent generations a barrier to violence and also to reproduction. He says, "The tendency on the part of civilization to restrict sexual life is no less clear than its other tendency to expand the cultural unit. Its first, totemic, phase already brings with it the prohibition against an incestuous choice of object, and this is perhaps the most drastic mutilation which man's erotic life has in all time experienced."[12] We, or the male among us, internalize the threats and prohibitions represented in the murdered father. On one hand, this internalization imposes a secondary nature on the human self, one that is neither happy in its origins nor able to be fully reconciled to the profounder pull of instinct. On the other hand it establishes the terms of collective life, the necessary truce that permits civilization to exist, and the sublimations by which civilization is distinguished. Freud's highly polished, deeply troubled Vienna, for many years seeming to sustain a perilous equilibrium between the strict imperatives of social order and the raw frictions of group conflict, bears more than a little resemblance to the Freudian self. To hope for more, for something to compare with the rootedness and authenticity for which the racial nationalists yearned, would risk destabilizing the very fragile equilibrium that for Freud is the closest approach human beings can make to their natural condition.

*

Figures such as Freud and Nietzsche, viewed against a background void of detail, seem to us to appear like meteors, to be singularities that shape intellectual space and time, not at all to have been shaped by them. Yet they are both inevitably engrossed in the passions that were consuming Europe. I have mentioned Fichte, Maurras, and Spengler as among the writers against whose influence Freud's metapsychological essays are directed. In general we Americans prefer to notice those thinkers we can find a way to admire, those whose thinking might enlarge our own, or refine it. This may possibly, on balance, be to our credit, I suppose. But there is the fact of modern history, and there is the fact that intellectuals, renowned in their time, made significant contributions to the worst of it. Freud, living in the midst of an emerging collective pathology as febrile in the universities as it was in the streets, could not have anticipated our highly selective indifference and admiration.

Fichte's reputation among us now is based on the philosophical texts that associate him with Kant. His *Addresses to the German Nation,* which were influential in the early formation of the theory of European nationalism, seem to be available in English only as a reprint of a damaged nineteenth-century copy of the book.[13] Charles Maurras, a vociferous anti-Semite about whose importance there is no doubt whatever, appears as a subject in studies of the extreme right in France, but little of his work is in translation. Spengler is available, but he and his book have dropped out of the conversation. So the context I assume for Freud, radically incomplete as it is, might seem a little recherche.

Fichte's *Addresses,* published at the beginning of the nineteenth century, when Germany had been successfully invaded by the armies of Napoleon, undertook to encourage a sense of the uniqueness of German-speaking peoples and to inspire loyalty to "the German Nation," which was then still many years away from unification and nationhood. He based his argument on the language they shared, which conferred on them a profundity and a capacity for truth that the mongrelized, Latinate French tongue could not approach. German being an original language, it was given to their nation by God, and therefore gave them privileged access to truth. "The investigations of a people with a living language go down, as we have already said, to the root where ideas stream forth from spiritual nature itself; whereas the investigations of a people with a dead language only seek to penetrate a foreign idea and to make themselves comprehensible. Hence, the investigations of the latter are in fact only historical and expository, but those of the former are truly philosophical."[14]

To adopt another language, or to allow an original language to be contaminated by foreign influence, was to be alienated from oneself at the cost of the most essential human qualities, and at the cost of spiritual wholeness and peace. This is an early version of the interpretation of European experience that made the contact and interpenetration of cultures the source of the individual and collective unhappiness acknowledged on every side. Though the French are, understandably, the irritant in this case, the concept is entirely open to being applied to foreigners and foreign influence in general. Though Fichte allows for the possibility of true linguistic assimilation, short of that the most loyal and well-intended immigrant population is as great a threat to true national survival as an invading army. This is a version of the logic behind the role of philology in racial nationalism.

Fichte's nationalism is a generous passion, given his view of history. He tells the German nation, "If there is truth in what has been expounded in these addresses, then are you of all modern peoples the one in whom the seed of human perfection most unmistakably lies, and to whom the lead in its development is committed. If you perish in this your essential nature, then there perishes together with you every hope of the whole human race for salvation from the depths of its miseries. . . . There is, therefore, no way out; if you go under, all humanity goes under with you, without hope of any future restoration."[15] The terrors and passions that lie behind these philosophies go much further than the philosophies themselves in anticipating and accounting for the extremes of modern European history.

When Oswald Spengler addresses the relationship of Jewish and European populations, he is rather evenhanded, by the standards of the time. But he, too, sees culture and history as the source of profound malaise. He dismisses "the silly catchwords 'Aryan' and 'Semite' that have been borrowed from philology." According to him the differences are between the old Jewish or Magian mind and the Gothic or Faustian mind, which is younger or at least slower maturing into the ways of civilization. But the consequences of this mingling of peoples, the inevitable mutual provocations, are the same, finally, as they always are in these narratives. "If there is inward relationship, a man affirms even where he destroys; if inward alienness, his effect is negative even where his desire is to be constructive. What Western Culture has destroyed, by reform efforts of its own type where it has had power, hardly bears thinking of; and Jewry has been equally destructive where it has intervened. The sense of the inevitableness of this reciprocal misunderstanding leads to the appalling hatred that settles deep in the blood and, fastening upon visible marks like race, mode of life, profession, speech, leads both sides to waste, ruin and bloody excesses wherever these conditions occur." Again, mingled with the magisterial philosophy of history we find the language of terrible fear. If I am correct in interpreting Freud's metapsychological writing, also in its way magisterial, it is an attempt to retell the narrative of European civilization, to counter the elements in prevailing narratives that provoked enmity and the sense of mortal threat. This is certainly an impulse consistent with his role as healer of the psyche, at least in the sense of maintaining its discomforts at the level of neurosis rather than seeing them flare into full-blown psychosis.[16]

Freud does speak to this grand malaise in the terms of its exponents. He says,

> When we consider how successful we have been in precisely this field of prevention of suffering, a suspicion dawns on us that here, too, a piece of unconquerable nature may lie behind—this time a piece of our own psychical condition.
>
> When we start considering this possibility, we come upon a contention which is so astonishing that we must dwell upon it. This contention holds that what we call our civilization is largely responsible for our misery, and that we should be much happier if we gave it up and

returned to primitive conditions. I call this contention astonishing because, in whatever way we may define the concept of civilization, it is a certain fact that all the things with which we seek to protect ourselves against the threats that emanate from the sources of suffering are part of that very civilization.[17]

*

It is a canard, and also true, that metaphysics as traditionally practiced has passed out of Western thought. Its abandonment is treated as one of those threshold events it is usual to proclaim, as if metaphysics were a naive exercise which we are now too knowing to persist in. As usual, where exactly this threshold is to be found varies with the telling. If I had to propose a date for the event, a moment in which this old habit was put aside, I would say it occurred when European thought turned from epistemology and ontology to politics and parascience—and when Freud was creating his great narrative about the nature of the mind. The exponents of the racial and nationalist theories meant to raise political and territorial passions to the high dignity of philosophy. Freud meant to bring passions and aversions under the cool scrutiny of science. The *Oxford English Dictionary* defines metaphysics as "that branch of speculative inquiry which treats of the first principles of things, including such concepts as being, substance, essence, time, space, cause, identity, etc.;

theoretical philosophy as the ultimate science of Being and Knowing."[18]

In the moment when science seemed to justify an insistence that the true could only be the objectively demonstrable, when science as a speculative art was still new enough that Spengler could describe relativity theory as "a ruthlessly cynical hypothesis," the rejection of metaphysics no doubt seemed rigorous and clarifying.[19] It was, in any case, of a piece with the rejection of religion as a repository of truth or of insight into the nature of humankind and our place in the universe, both of these questions being shifted into the language of science as that word was then understood.

I will put aside for the moment whether or not the concepts the dictionary identifies as metaphysical can indeed be excluded from statements about human nature. Freud's account of human origins goes very far toward describing an anti-metaphysics, proposing an encapsulated self with as few ties to a larger reality as are consistent with its survival. According to Freud's account of biological origins in *Beyond the Pleasure Principle,* in embryonic development the integument folds inward to form the nervous system, and this fact accounts for the character of consciousness. "Indeed embryology, in its capacity as a recapitulation of developmental history, actually shows us that the central nervous system originates from the ectoderm; the grey matter of the cortex remains a derivative of the primitive superficial layer of the organism and may have inherited some of its essential properties." Here is how he expands this observation.

> This little fragment of living substance [the simplest type of organism] is suspended in the middle of an external world charged with the most powerful energies; and it would be killed by the stimulation emanating from these if it were not provided with a protective shield against stimuli. It acquires the shield in this way: its outermost surface ceases to have the structure proper to living matter, becomes to some degree inorganic and thenceforward functions as a special envelope or membrane resistant to stimuli. . . . *Protection against* stimuli is an almost more important function for the living organism than *reception* of stimuli. . . . The main purpose of the *reception* of stimuli is to discover the direction and nature of the external stimuli; and for that it is enough to take small specimens of the external world, to sample it in small quantities.[20]

This little entity, "threatened by the enormous energies at work in the external world," forms a "crust" to defend itself against, in effect, experience. Freud offers this fable to suggest that "the exposed situation of the system *Cs.*, immediately abutting as it does on the external world," might account for its difference from other mental systems.[21] However limited his intention, however, Freud has proposed a very strange and powerful model of reality, one in which the world in itself is an intolerable threat, and only the strict rationing of awareness of it, by grace of the selectivity of the senses, makes the organism able to endure it.

Considered over against, let us say, Romanticism, or any mode of thought or belief that proposed an intuitive contact with profound reality as possible and normative, and even against the very unspecific "oceanic feeling" which his colleague Romain Rolland asked him to acknowledge and about which he wrote in *Civilization and Its Discontents,* Freud's model of the origins and nature of consciousness is of a being first of all besieged and beleaguered, not by the threats posed by the vital, amoral energies of Darwinian nature, but by, so to speak, the cosmos, the barrage of undifferentiated stimuli which is everything that is not oneself.

Freud defines the "oceanic feeling" as "a feeling of an indissoluble bond, of being one with the external world as a whole." He speaks about this notion as if there had never been such a thing as Romanticism, as if Fichte or Maurras or Spengler had never pined for a lost bond with the earth. He says, "The idea of men's receiving an intimation of their connection with the world around them through an immediate feeling which is from the outset directed to that purpose sounds so strange and fits in so badly with the fabric of our psychology that one is justified in attempting to discover a psycho-analytic—that is, a genetic—explanation of such a feeling." That he should speak dismissively of "such a feeling" at the beginning of *Civilization and Its Discontents,* when so many of his contemporaries laid those discontents to the loss of what Spengler calls "the beat" of authentic life, that he should express amazement at the notion and disallow the meaningfulness of this feeling on firm scientific grounds, is certainly understandable as a rhetorical or polemical strategy. He says, making unmistakable the consequences of viewing this "intimation" in the light of science, "pathology has made us acquainted with a great number of states in which the boundary lines between the ego and the external world become uncertain or in which they are actually drawn incorrectly."[22]

I am suggesting here that Freud was part of an odd, post-metaphysical conversation, an early instance of a conversation that is uniquely modern. On one side "profundity" refers to the imagined beneficial consequences for individual and group consciousness of ethnic or cultural purity, a state projected into a mythic past and then treated as the one true reality, against which present reality is weighed and found wanting. On the other side, Freud's side, consciousness is in its nature both threatened by and shielded from contact with an external world which he nowhere represents as friendly to our presence in it or as capable of imparting to us authenticity, truth, meaning, profundity, or anything else of a presumably positive character. Both sides curtail the dimensions of traditional Western thought radically, the reactionary position by conforming it to an extreme, fearful, and nostalgic politics, and Freud's position by insisting on a psychology that withdraws itself from history, from culture in the narrow sense, and from the natural world as well. Neither argument has much to recommend it. Crucially, both represent the mind as, for one reason or another, not to be credited.

Descartes anchored his argument for an objective and knowable reality in the fact of the experience of his own mind thinking. He assumed that in thought he bore the kind of relation to God that made his consciousness in its nature a conduit of true perception. Therefore, so his argument goes, science is possible, the world is knowable, and experience, which for him meant the kind of truth sought out by the methods of science, is authorized by God himself. This is an argument directed against the belief that science and its methods were irreligious. It is, necessarily, also dependent on a metaphysics that assumes a God with whom humanity bears an essential likeness and kinship. Granting all the assumptions implicit in the fact that it was through disciplined inquiry that the world could be known—that is, that knowledge of reality was hard-won—nevertheless, with all caveats acknowledged that science acknowledges, the mind can be trusted, according to Descartes.

If there is one thing Freud asserts consistently, from which every theory proceeds and to which every conclusion returns, it is just this—that the mind is *not* to be trusted. The conversation in the larger culture to which I have referred, the variously lamented loss of spiritual authenticity, assumes that civilization has alienated Europeans from their essential selves and corrupted their experience. But at least the sense of alienation is to be credited as a true report on their condition, and the integrity of mind of which they believe they have been deprived they also believe can be restored to them. For Freud, self-alienation is a consequence of human ontogeny. Freud's "sexual theory," in generalizing the sexual so thoroughly, renders that concept as nearly meaningless as the concept of culture which the theory does indeed undermine. For the purposes of the metapsychological essays, the theory makes sexuality primarily a name for the urges of the involuted self, the unacknowledged core of archaic frustration and guilt at the center of subjective experience which baffles and misleads conscious awareness.

Freud's self is encapsulated, engrossed by an interior drama of which it cannot be consciously aware—unless instructed in self-awareness by means of psychoanalysis. That is to say, the center of emotional experience, the source of motive and inhibition, is inaccessible to the self as experience. The consciousness, whose ignorance of motive and inhibition is an accommodation to the demands of civilization, is therefore false, and civilization, the sum total of such accommodation, is false as well. If this conclusion was shocking to Jung, it is, nevertheless, a Freudian understanding of a state of things very widely attested to, an understanding that saw a painfully achieved equilibrium where others saw decline and dissolution, that saw in unrest the inescapable fate that is individual and collective human nature rather than corruption, evil, and subversion, which were taken to be alien or Jewish in their sources. Why a vision of man and society so specific to an extraordinary historical circumstance should have been universalized as for many years it was is an interesting question. Freud's brilliance was surely a factor, as well as the high status of the culture of which he was so earnestly and uneasily a part, even after it expelled him. Considered aright, his metapsychology might be seen as the testimony of a singular observer to the emotional stresses of life in a fracturing civilization. It might be seen as a gloss on the fact that grand theories of human nature, however magisterial, can be based only on encounters with the world in circumstances that are always exceptional because the factors in play are always too novel, numerous, and volatile to permit generalization. In his role as scientist, which by the standards of the time he had every right to assert, Freud tried to bring the assumptions of rationalism to bear on the myths and frenzies that were carrying Europe toward catastrophe. In the event, he brought to bear not reason but rationalization, treating the Europe of his time as timeless and normative, and therefore, in its fractious way, stable. Notably, he attempted to redefine the unconscious, a concept then broadly associated with primitive racial and national identity, making it instead a force in a universal yet radically interior dynamic of self. Granting the perils of delusion, fear, denial, and all the other excesses to which the mind is prone, this severely narrow construction of the mind, suspicious of every impulse and motive that does not seem to express the few but potent urges of the primitive self, bears the mark of its time. Yet, perhaps because of its superficial affinity to social Darwinist and then neo-Darwinist assumptions, it continues to hold its place among the great, sad, epochal insights that we say have made us modern.

# FOUR

# Thinking Again

I t will be a great day in the history of science if we sometime discover a damp shadow elsewhere in the universe where a fungus has sprouted. The mere fossil trace of life in its simplest form would be the crowning achievement of generations of brilliant and diligent labor. And here we are, a gaudy efflorescence of consciousness, staggeringly improbable in light of everything we know about the reality that contains us. There are physicists and philosophers who would correct me. They would say, if there are an infinite number of universes, as in theory there could be, then creatures like us would be very likely to emerge at some time in one of them. But to say this is only to state the fact of our improbability in other terms.

Then there is the odd privilege of existence as a coherent self, the ability to speak the word "I" and mean by it a richly individual history of experience, perception, and thought. For the religious, the sense of the soul may have as a final redoubt, not as argument but as experience, that haunting I who wakes us in the night wondering where time has gone, the I we waken to, sharply aware that we have been unfaithful to ourselves, that a life lived otherwise would have acknowledged a yearning more our own than any of the daylit motives whose behests we answer to so diligently. Our religious traditions give us as the name of God two deeply mysterious words, one deeply mysterious utterance: I AM. Putting to one side the question of their meaning as the name and character by which the God of Moses would be known, these are words any human being can say about herself, and does say, though always with a modifier of some kind. I am hungry, I am comfortable, I am a singer, I am a cook. The abrupt descent into particularity in every statement of this kind, Being itself made an auxiliary to some momentary accident of being, may only startle in the dark of night, when the intuition comes that there is no proportion between the great given of existence and the narrow vessel of circumstance into which it is inevitably forced. "I am Ozymandias, king of kings. Look on my works, ye mighty, and despair."

There is much speculation about the nature of the mind, its relation to the brain, even doubt that the word "mind" is meaningful. According to E. O. Wilson, "The brain and its satellite glands have now been probed to the point where no particular site remains that can reasonably be supposed to harbor a nonphysical mind." Perhaps this statement is to be taken as tongue-in-cheek. But to prove a negative, or to treat it as having been proved, is, oddly enough, an old and essential strategy of positivism. So I do feel obliged to point out that if such a site could be found in the brain, then the mind would be physical in the same sense that anything else with a locus in the brain is physical. To define the mind as nonphysical in the first place clearly prejudices his conclusion. Steven Pinker, on the soul, asks, "How does the spook interact with solid matter? How does an ethereal nothing respond to flashes, pokes and beeps and get arms and legs to move? Another problem is the overwhelming evidence that the mind is the activity of the brain. The supposedly immaterial soul, we now know, can be bisected with a knife, altered by chemicals," and so on. By identifying the soul with the mind, the mind with the brain, and noting the brain's vulnerability as a physical object, he feels he has debunked a conception of the soul that only those who find the word meaningless would ever have entertained.[1]

This declension, from the ethereality of the mind/soul as spirit to the reality of the mind/brain as a lump of meat, is dependent, conceptually and for its effects, on precisely the antique dualism these writers who claim to speak for science believe they reject and refute. If complex life is the marvel we all say it is, quite possibly unique to this planet, then meat is, so to speak, that marvel in its incarnate form. It was dualism that pitted the spirit against the flesh, investing spirit with all that is lofty at the expense of flesh, which is by contrast understood as coarse and base. It only perpetuates dualist thinking to treat the physical as if it were in any way sufficiently described in disparaging terms. If the mind is the activity of the brain, this means only that the brain is capable of such lofty and astonishing things that their expression has been given the names mind, and soul, and spirit. Complex life may well be the wonder of the universe, and if it is, its status is not diminished by the fact that we can indeed bisect it, that we kill it routinely.

In any case, Wilson's conception of mind clearly has also taken on the properties of the soul, at least as that entity is understood by those eager to insist that there is no ghost in the machine. As Bertrand Russell pointed out decades before Gilbert Ryle coined this potent phrase, the old, confident distinction between materiality and nonmateriality is not a thing modern science can endorse. Physicists say a change in a split photon occurs simultaneously in its severed half, at any theoretical distance. As if there were no time or space, this information of change passes instantly from one to the other. Is an event that defies any understanding we have of causality a physical event? Yes. Can the seeming timelessness and spacelessness that mediate this change also be called physical? Presumably, since they have unambiguous physical consequences. Then perhaps we cannot claim to know the nature of the physical, and perhaps we ought not to be so confident in opposing it to a real or imagined nonphysical. These terms, as conventionally used, are not identical with the terms "real" and "unreal," though the belief that they are is the oldest tenet of positivism. The old notion of dualism should be put aside, now that we know a little about the uncanny properties of the finer textures of the physical. If, as some have suggested, quantum phenomena govern the brain, evidence for the fact is not likely to be found in scrutiny of lobes or glands or by means of any primitive understanding of the brain's materiality.

Let us say the mind is what the brain does. This is a definition that makes the mind, whatever else, a participant in the whole history and experience of the body. (Steven Pinker offers the same definition, but modifies it differently.

He says, "The mind is what the brain does; specifically, the brain processes information, and thinking is a kind of computation"—excluding the felt experience of thinking, with all its diverse burdens and colorations.) Elsewhere he says, with the certitude typical of his genre, "Family feelings are designed to help our genes replicate themselves, but we cannot see or smell genes. . . . Our emotions about kin use a kind of inverse genetics to guess which of the organisms we interact with are likely to share our genes (for example, if someone appears to have the same parents as you do, treat the person as if their genetic well-being overlaps with yours)."[2] And again we have the self we experience at a qualitative remove from what the brain really does. Presumably we are seduced into collaborating in the perpetuation of some part of our genetic inheritance by those moments of love and embrace. But why are these seductions necessary? Why are they lovely to us? Why would nature bother to distract us with them? Why do we stand apart from nature in such a way that the interests that really move us should be concealed from us? Might there not be fewer of these interfamilial crimes, honor killings, child abandonments, if nature had made us straightforwardly aware that urgencies more or less our own were being served in our propagating and nurturing? There is more than a hint of dualism in the notion that some better self—the term seems fair—has to be distracted by ingratiating pleasures to accommodate the practical business of biology.

This automaton language of Pinker's sounds a bit like Descartes. But Descartes theorized that the pineal gland, central and singular in the symmetries of the brain, moved one way or another to permit or obstruct the actions of the body, which he knew were governed by the brain. In his theory, the impressions of the senses, integrated in this gland, were appraised by the soul, which in Descartes is a term that seems pointedly synonymous with the mind. That is to say, his interest is in cognition and reason, not sin or salvation, and this in a physical and intellectual landscape inflamed by theological controversy in which those concepts figured prominently. Still, it is the soul that appraises what the mind integrates. In this way Descartes acknowledges the complexity of thinking, judging, and in his way incorporates the feeling of consciousness and the complexity of it more adequately than most theorists do now. He speaks of the mind, which he calls "I, that is to say, the mind by which I am what I am," in ways that assume it is nevertheless accessible to instruction and correction by an I that stands apart from it.[3] To correct the syntax of his thinking so that the anomaly is removed would be to deprive it of its power as testimony— we do indeed continuously stand apart from ourselves, appraising. Every higher act of the mind, intellectual, aesthetic, or moral, is, paradoxically, also an exercise in self-doubt, self-scrutiny.

What Descartes actually intended by the words "soul" and "mind" seems to me an open question for Descartes himself. Clearly they are no mere ghost or illusion. No doubt there are volumes to be consulted on this subject. What their meanings are for us as inheritors of the thought of the modern period is a more manageable question. I am excluding the kind of thinking on this point that tends toward the model of the wager. According to this model, we place our faith in an understanding of the one thing needful, and, ultimately, suffer or triumph depending on the correctness of our choice. By these lights the soul exists primarily to be saved or lost. It is hardly more our intimate companion in mortal time than is the mind or brain by the reckoning of the positivists, behaviorists, neo-Darwinists, and Freudians. The soul, in this understanding of it, is easily characterized by the nonreligious as a fearful and self-interested idea, as the product of acculturation or a fetish of the primitive brain rather than as a name for an aspect of deep experience. Therefore it is readily dismissed as a phantom of the mind, and the mind is all the more readily dismissed for its harboring of such fears and delusions.

Descartes complains that "the philosophers of the

schools accept as a maxim that there is nothing in the under-standing which was not previously in the senses." The stric-tures of this style of thought are indeed very old. It strikes me that the word "senses" is in need of definition. As it is used, even by these schoolmen, it seems to signify only those means by which we take in information about our environment, including our own bodies, presumably. Steven Pinker says, "The faculty with which we ponder the world has no ability to peer inside itself or our other faculties to see what makes them tick. That makes us the victims of an illusion: that our own psychology comes from some divine force or mysterious es-sence or almighty principle."[4] But the mind, or the brain, a part of the body just as Wilson says it is, is deeply sensitive to itself. Guilt, nostalgia, the pleasure of anticipation, even the shock of a realization, all arise out of an event that occurs entirely in the mind or brain, and they are as potent as other sensations. Consistency would require a belief in the non-physical character of the mind to exclude them from the general category of experience. If it is objected that all these things are ultimately dependent on images and sensations first gleaned from the world by the senses, this might be granted, on the condition that the sensory experience re-tained in the mind is understood to have the character the mind has given it. And it might be granted if sensory experi-ence is understood to function as language does, both enabling thought and conforming it in large part to its own context, its own limitations. Anyone's sensory experience of the world is circumstantial and cultural, qualified by context and perspective, a fact which again suggests that the mind's awareness of itself is of a kind with its awareness of physical reality. The mind, like the body, is very much placed in the world. Those who claim to dismiss the mind/body dichotomy actually perpetuate it when they exclude the mind's self-awareness from among the data of human nature.

By "self-awareness" I do not mean merely consciousness of one's identity, or of the complex flow of thought, perception, memory, and desire, important as these are. I mean primarily the self that stands apart from itself, that questions, reconsiders, appraises. I have read that microorganisms can equip themselves with genes useful to their survival —that is, genes conferring resistance to antibiotics—by choosing them out of the ambient flux of organic material. This is not a pretty metaphor, but it makes a point. If a supposedly simple entity can by any means negotiate its own enhancement, then an extremely complex entity, largely composed of these lesser entities—that is, a human being—should be assumed to have analogous capabilities. For the purposes of the mind, these might be called conscience or aspiration. We receive their specific forms culturally and historically, as the microorganism, our contemporary, does also when it absorbs the consequences of other germs' encounters with the human pharmacopoeia. Let us say that social pathologies can be associated with traumatic injuries to certain areas of the brain, and that the unimpaired brain has the degree of detachment necessary to report to us when our behavior might be, as they say in the corrections community, inappropriate. Then what grounds can there be for doubting that a sufficient biological account of the brain would yield the complex phenomenon we know and experience as the mind? It is only the pertinacity of the mind/body dichotomy that sustains the notion that a sufficient biological account of the brain would be reductionist in the negative sense. Such thinking is starkly at odds with our awareness of the utter brilliance of the physical body.

I do not myself believe that such an account of the brain will ever be made. Present research methods show the relatively greater activity of specific regions of the brain in response to certain stimuli or in the course of certain mental or physical behaviors. But in fact it hardly seems possible that in practice the region of the brain that yields speech would not be deeply integrated with the regions that govern social behavior as well as memory and imagination, to degrees varying with circumstances. Nor does it seem possible that each of these would not under all circumstances profoundly modify the others, in keeping with learning and with inherited and other qualities specific to any particular brain. What should we call the presiding intelligence that orchestrates the decision to speak as a moment requires? What governs the inflections that make any utterance unmistakably the words of one speaker in this whole language-saturated world? To say it is the brain is insufficient, over-general, implying nothing about nuance and individuation. Much better to call it the mind.

If the brain at the level of complex and nuanced interaction with itself does indeed become mind, then the reductionist approach insisted upon by writers on the subject is not capable of yielding evidence of mind's existence, let alone an account of its functioning. One who has inquired into the properties of hydrogen and oxygen might reasonably conclude that water is a highly combustible gas—if there were not his own experience to discourage this conclusion. As proof of the existence of mind we have only history and civilization, art, science, and philosophy. And at the same time, of course, that extraordinary individuation. If it is true that the mind can know and seek to know itself in ways analogous to its experience of the world, then there are more, richer data to be gleaned from every age and every culture, and from every moment of introspection, of deep awareness of the self.

To return briefly to the notion of multiverses. There is no

reason I am aware of to doubt that our known reality is one of an endless number of realities, most of them ephemeral and unhaunted, presumably, though that is speculation. This hypothesis is so convenient to those who wish to minimize the significance of the apparent fine-tuning of our universe to allow for the existence of life, and so inaccessible to disproof, that there is something a little comical about it. Still, lifted out of the polemical context in which it is often to be found, the notion seems plausible enough. Why should there be, or have been, only one great singularity, one great surge of cosmos? Our universe is sufficient to prepare our imaginations for plenitude on an even grander scale.

So, granting the plausibility of the idea, what does it imply? Its power, when it is used polemically, is based on the fact that, in a multiverse, absolutely anything is possible. Take that, Reverend Paley. Still, it does draw attention to the givenness, the arbitrariness, one might even say the narrowness, of the protocols that govern our reality. Everything we take to be essential could be the accident of a peculiar history, a warp or an asymmetry in this one emergence that eventuated as time, or as gravity. To say that everything could be utterly different from universe to universe itself suggests infinite variants on a substructure of reality whose existence it is surely an error to assume. If it would still be meaningful to say, There are an infinite number of universes—if their profound otherness did not embarrass even the language of Being itself—then our own experience of Being is obviously far too minor and partial to support generalization. If something we could discern and recognize as intelligent life were to occur in certain of these other realities, might we not learn that our notions of intelligence were, so to speak, parochial? Might we not reconsider our ideas of intelligence as it occurs here on earth? If the question seems fanciful, the use if not the point of the multiverse hypothesis is precisely to enlarge or even to explode conventional and restrictive notions of the possible. My point is simply that the ancient assumption of parascience, that we are playing with a full deck, that we can proceed from an understanding of reality that is in every important sense sufficient, is a feature of the literature carried forward from a primitive notion of what sufficiency would be.

On one hand we have the most ancient and universal theological intuition, that the order we see exists by divine fiat, that the heavens proclaim the glory of God. And on the other hand we have this late development in cosmological speculation, the notion that the reality we experience is arbitrary, being one manifestation of an infinitely greater potentiality. I run the risk here of seeming to theologize science or to use scientific speculation to vindicate theology. This is true only in that, in both cases, the sense of the arbitrariness of given reality allows the human mind to see around its edges, so to speak—to acknowledge the potential in the interstices of the actual. To clarify this point I will quote a sharply contrasting view, expressed by E. O. Wilson in the last chapter of his book *On Human Nature,* published in 1979. "The core of scientific materialism is the evolutionary epic. Let me repeat its minimum claims: that the laws of the physical sciences are consistent with those of the biological and social sciences and can be linked in chains of causal explanation; that life and mind have a physical basis; that the world as we know it has evolved from earlier worlds obedient to the same laws; and that the visible universe today is everywhere subject to these materialist explanations."[5]

I confess to finding this language unclear. I think I am fair to Wilson in taking him to mean that the physical and social sciences are coextensive, and that the laws of the first can therefore be presumed to govern the second, at least in principle or by extension, a notion already asserted in the nineteenth century by Auguste Comte. What this would mean in practice is still difficult to imagine, however, even putting to one side the question of whether the social sciences are in fact sciences, or are methodical and testable enough to identify in themselves the workings of the kinds of apparently universal constants it is customary to call "laws." I take it to mean that this world has passed through states of evolution, each of which would have been comprehensible in the terms of our understanding of, in Wilson's phrase, "the visible universe." A fair amount has happened in science since the publication of this book in 1979. We now know that only a small fraction of the universe is in any sense visible, that the adjective "dark" is now applied to most of it, meaning that the presence of unanticipated forms of matter and energy can be discerned or inferred though not "explained."

Of course these must be assumed to be in principle "subject to materialist explanations," though I would rephrase this as "available to tentative description in terms science finds meaningful." But these phenomena demonstrate, as physics and cosmology tend to do, that the strangeness of reality consistently exceeds the expectations of science, and that the assumptions of science, however tried and rational, are very inclined to encourage false expectations. As a notable example, no one expected to find that the expansion of the universe is accelerating, and that the rate of its acceleration is accelerating. It is a tribute to the brilliance of science that we can know such things. And it is also an illustration of the fact that science does not foreclose possibility, including discoveries that overturn very fundamental assumptions, and that it is not a final statement about reality but a highly fruitful mode of inquiry into it.

The fact of the accelerating expansion of the universe is

a conclusion arrived at in the first place by observation. Theory and hypothesis have followed. What was thought to be known about the effect of gravity, that it would slow cosmic expansion, could not be reconciled with new data, and a major and novel factor, in effect an antigravitational force, emerged as a hypothesis in a changed conception of the universe. The best wisdom and the most venerable of natural laws do not have standing to preclude our acknowledging solid data, though the grounds for refusing to take account of them could perfectly well be called "scientific." The exclusion of what the brain does from an account of what the brain is is "scientific" in just the same sense. By this kind of reasoning, the laws of nature supposedly tell us what we must exclude from what we might otherwise consider entirely relevant, one example being our own inwardness. This distinction between science and "science" is important in considering the mind over against the materialist position that would understand it in reductionist terms, that is, in terms that limit the kinds of interpretation that are appropriately brought to bear on it. The neo-Darwinists argue that the brain evolved to maximize the chance of genetic survival, to negotiate access to food and sex, presumably before the species evolved to the point where the prolonged helplessness of infants made genetic survival dependent in some degree on cooperation. Therefore, they tell us, we may not assume that any motive can depart from an essential qualitative likeness to these original motives. The "evolutionary epic" explains the brain exhaustively.

But "the material" itself is an artifact of the scale at which we perceive. We know that we abide with quarks and constellations, in a reality unknowable by us in a degree we will never be able to calculate, but reality all the same, the stuff and the matrix of our supposedly quotidian existence. We know that within, throughout, the solid substantiality of our experience indeterminacy reigns. Making use of the conceptual vocabulary of science to exclude a possibility that in a present state of knowledge—or a former one—that vocabulary would seem to exclude, has been the mission of positivist thinking since Auguste Comte declared scientific knowledge effectively complete. If doing so is a reflex of the polemical impulse to assert the authority of science, understandable when the project was relatively new, it is by now an atavism that persists as a consequence of this same polemical impulse.

The ancient antagonist that has shaped positivism and parascientific thought and continues to inspire its missionary zeal is religion. For cultural and historical reasons, the religions against which it has opposed itself are Christianity and Judaism, both of which must be called anthropologies, whatever else. "What is man that thou art mindful of him?" The very question is an assertion that mindfulness is an attribute of God, as well as man, a statement of the sense of deep meaning inhering in mindfulness. If I were not myself a religious person, but wished to make an account of religion, I believe I would tend toward the Feuerbachian view that religion is a human projection of humanity's conceptions of beauty, goodness, power, and other valued things, a humanizing of experience by understanding it as structured around and mirroring back these values. Then it would resemble art, with which it is strongly associated. But this would dignify religion and characterize the mind as outwardly and imaginatively engaged with the world, as, in parascientific thought after Comte, it never is. Sigmund Freud, in *Civilization and Its Discontents*, says of religion, "The whole thing is so patently infantile, so foreign to reality, that to anyone with a friendly attitude to humanity it is painful to think that the great majority of mortals will never be able to rise above this view of life." Then, two pages on, he says, "The question of the purpose of human life has been raised countless times: it has never received a satisfactory answer and perhaps does not admit of one. . . . Once again, only religion can answer the question of the purpose of life. One can hardly be wrong in concluding that the idea of life having a purpose stands and falls with the religious system." And then he says, "As we see, what decides the purpose of life is simply the programme of the pleasure principle. This principle dominates the operation of the mental apparatus from the start. There can be no doubt about its efficacy, and yet its programme is at loggerheads with the whole world, with the macrocosm as much as with the microcosm. There is no possibility at all of its being carried through; all the regulations of the universe run counter to it."[6]

It seems a little strange that religion is infantile but the desire for pleasure, which "dominates the operation of the mental apparatus from the start," is not, or not, at least, in any pejorative sense. It seems strange as well that though "there is no possibility at all of its being carried out," the programme of the pleasure principle is not also, like religion, "foreign to reality." Steven Pinker says, "Religion is a desperate measure that people resort to when the stakes are high and they have exhausted the usual techniques for the causation of success." Then a little farther on he lists the "imponderables" that lie behind the human tendency toward religion and also philosophy. These imponderables are consciousness in the sense of sentience or subjective experience, the self, free will, conceptual meaning, knowledge, and morality. He says, "Maybe philosophical problems are hard not because they are divine or irreducible or meaningless or workaday science, but because the mind of Homo sapiens lacks the cognitive equipment to solve them. We are organisms, not angels, and our brains are organs, not pipelines to the truth."[7]

How odd that these "imponderables" should be just the kind of thing humankind has pondered endlessly. Neo-Darwinism allows for hypertrophy, the phenomenon by which evolution overshoots its mark and produces some consequence not strictly useful to the ends of genetic replication, the human brain as case in point. How strange it would be, then, that this accident, this excess, should feel a tropism toward what Pinker himself calls "the truth."

The great difference between parascientific thought on one hand and religion and traditional philosophy on the other is perhaps encapsulated in that word "solve," assuming the use of the word is not simply a casual imprecision. It does seem as though, for the purposes of these writers, science is the conquest of mystery, as it was for Auguste Comte, and as it certainly was not for Isaac Newton. A difference between a Newton and a Comte, between science and parascience, is the desire in the latter case to treat scientific knowledge as complete, at least in its methods and assumptions, in order to further the primary object of closing questions about human nature and the human circumstance.

*

Science has arrived at a cluster of hypotheses about the first instant of creation. They attempt description, in the manner of science. In course of time, on various grounds, one description might prove to be more satisfactory than others. A consensus might be arrived at about the nature of a very fecund particle whose eruption became everything we know, and a great deal more beside. We might learn at some point whether time was created together with this universe or exists independently of it. The questions to which science in its most sophisticated forms has come would have been the imponderables of philosophy a few generations ago, of theology a few centuries ago, of religion a few millennia ago. Why this ancient instinct for the greatest questions? It is striking that Freud identifies religion with the meaning of life, and Pinker identifies it with the high-order questions humankind has posed to itself from antiquity. Then both writers for all purposes dismiss these things as insoluble, as if that were a legitimate reason to dismiss any question. We may never know why gravity is so much weaker than, in theory, it should be, or know if we are only one among any number of actual and potential universes. But every real question is fruitful, as the history of human thought so clearly demonstrates.

And "fruitful" is by no means a synonym for "soluble." What is man? One answer on offer is, An organism whose haunting questions perhaps ought not to be meaningful to the organ that generates them, lacking as it is in any means of "solving" them. Another answer might be, It is still too soon to tell. We might be the creature who brings life on this planet to an end, and we might be the creature who awakens to the privileges that inhere in our nature—selfhood, consciousness, even our biologically anomalous craving for "the truth"—and enjoys and enhances them. Mysteriously, neither possibility precludes the other. Our nature will describe itself as we respond to new circumstances in a world that changes continuously. So long as the human mind exists to impose itself on reality, as it has already done so profoundly, what it is and what we are must remain an open question.

In order to arrive at a parascientific view of humankind we are obliged to put to one side whatever is not to be accounted for in the apparently simple terms of genetic self-interest. I say "apparently simple" because in every instance these theorists build in devices to account for the inadequacies of their theories. The Ptolemaic model of the universe worked well enough, given certain cogs and wheels, epicycles and deferents. These theorists speak of the old error, that notion of a ghost in the machine, the image of the felt difference between mind and body. But who and what is that other self they posit, the hypertrophic self who has considered the heavens since Babylon and considers them still, by elegant and ingenious means whose refinements express a formidable pressure of desire to see and know far beyond the limits of any conception of utility, certainly any neo-Darwinist conception of it? Who is that other self needing to be persuaded that there are more than genetic reasons for rescuing a son or daughter from drowning? The archaic conundrum, how a nonphysical spirit can move a physical body, only emerges in a more pointed form in these unaccountable presences whom evolution has supposedly contrived to make us mistake for ourselves. These epigones exist because without them the theories would fail the test of comparison with human experience. Merely shift the balance toward manifest behavior, assuming that the genes do indeed look after themselves in ways and degrees we most likely cannot yet describe, but in any case that their functioning is consistent with manifest behavior. Then human nature, in its wholeness and complexity, is restored—as an unsolved problem, but as a phenomenon endlessly offering a very burdened testimony.

Each of us lives intensely within herself or himself, continuously assimilating past and present experience to a narrative and vision that are unique in every case yet profoundly communicable, whence the arts. And we all live in a great reef of collective experience, past and present, that we receive and preserve and modify. William James says data should be thought of not as givens but as gifts, this by way of maintaining an appropriate humility in the face of what we think we know. The gifts we bring to the problem of making an account of the mind are overwhelmingly rich, severally and together. This is not an excuse for excluding them from consideration. History and civilization are an authoritative record the mind has left, is leaving, and will leave, and objectivity deserving the name would take this record as a starting point. In practical terms, this would mean doing as the humanists have done since the building of the library of Alexandria, more or less. Humankind never ceases to express itself in new terms, and the data at hand are inevitably flawed and partial. But the complexity of the object, the human brain, and all associated phenomena are at the center of the question, inextricable from it. The schools of thought I have criticized exclude the great fact of human exceptionalism, though no one would deny that it is a pure expression of the uniqueness of the human brain.

A primary assumption of the evolutionary model behind neo-Darwinism is that development can be traced back through a series of subtly incremental changes. At what for our purposes is the terminus of all these changes there emerges, voila, the world as we know it. The neatness of this argument has always bothered me, but this is no refutation of it, nor am I interested in refuting it. I wish only to point out that there are certain things it should not be taken to imply. For example, it does not imply that a species carries forward an essential similarity to its ancestors. A bird is not a latter-day dinosaur. We can assume the ancestors ate and slept and mated, carrying on the universal business of animal life. Still,

whatever the shared genetic history of beast and bird, a transformative change occurred over the millennia, and to find the
modern sparrow implicit in the thunder lizard is quite certainly an error, if one wishes to make an ornithological study
of sparrow behavior. On the same grounds, there is no reason
to assume our species resembles in any essential way the
ancient primates whose genes we carry. It is a strategy of
parascientific argument to strip away culture-making, as if it
were a ruse and a concealment within which lurked the imagined primitive who is for them our true nature.

Here is another instance of evolution, to illustrate my
point. The universe passed through its unimaginable first
moment, first year, first billion years, wresting itself from
whatever state of nonexistence, inflating, contorting, resolv-
ing into space and matter, bursting into light. Matter con-
denses, stars live out their generations. Then, very late, there
is added to the universe of being a shaped stick or stone, a jug,
a cuneiform tablet. They appear on a tiny, teetering, lopsided
planet, and they demand wholly new vocabularies of description for reality at every scale. What but the energies of the
universe could be expressed in the Great Wall of China, the *St.
Matthew Passion*? For our purposes, there *is* nothing else. Yet
language that would have been fully adequate to describe the
ages before the appearance of the first artifact would have had
to be enlarged by concepts like agency and intention, words

like creation, that would query the great universe itself. Might not the human brain, that most complex object known to exist in the universe, have undergone a qualitative change as well? If my metaphor only suggests the possibility that our species is more than an optimized ape, that something terrible and glorious befell us, a change gradualism could not predict—if this is merely another fable, it might at least encourage an imagination of humankind large enough to acknowledge some small fragment of the mystery we are.

ONE  *On Human Nature*

1. Santiago Zabala, introduction to Rorty and Vattimo, *Future of Religion*.
2. Balthasar, *Presence and Thought*, 1.
3. Rorty and Vattimo, *Future of Religion*, 17.
4. James, "On Some Hegelisms" in his *Will to Believe.*
5. James, *Varieties of Religious Experience*, 42 (emphasis in original).
6. Dennett, *Breaking the Spell*, 9, 11; Russell, *Analysis of Mind*, 230.
7. Russell, *Why I Am Not a Christian*, 27.
8. Ibid., 7.
9. Bonhoeffer, *Letters and Papers from Prison*, 359.

10. Russell, *Analysis of Mind,* 236.

11. Pinker, *Blank Slate,* 56–57. See Patrick Tierney, *Darkness in El Dorado: How Scientists and Journalists Devastated the Amazon* (New York: W. W. Norton, 2000), and Robert Borofsky, *Yanomami: The Fierce Controversy and What We Can Learn From It* (Los Angeles: University of California Press, 2005).

12. Pinker, *Blank Slate,* 56.

13. Ibid., 69.

14. Pinker, *Blank Slate,* 42.

15. Kugel, *How to Read the Bible,* 80.

16. Grotius, *On the Truth of the Christian Religion,* 11.

17. Ibid., 13.

18. See James, *Varieties of Religious Experience,* 389, note 10.

T W O  *The Strange History of Altruism*

1. Auguste Comte, A *General View of Positivism,* trans. J. H. Bridges (London: Trübner, 1865), 34.

2. Ibid., 16.

3. *Encyclopaedia Britannica,* 11th ed., s.v. "Comte, Auguste (Isidore Auguste Marie François Xavier)"; James, "On Some Hegelisms," in his *Will to Believe,* 198, note 3.

4. Spencer, *Data of Ethics,* 188–189, 201–202.

5. Gazzaniga, *Human,* 107–108, 109.

6. Ibid., 119.

7. Ibid., 119; Damasio, *Descartes' Error,* 56, 33.

8. Wilson, *Consilience,* 96–97.

9. James, "On Some Hegelisms," 201.

10. Wilson, *On Human Nature,* 73.

11. Ibid., 156; Gazzaniga, *Human,* 106 (parentheses in original);

Steven Pinker, *How the Mind Works* (New York: W. W. Norton, 2009), 44.

12. Spencer, *Data of Ethics,* 212. See Dugatkin, *Altruism Equation,* 86–106, for a discussion of Hamilton's work.

13. See Dugatkin, *Altruism Equation,* 143–146.

14. Ibid., 73.

15. Quoted in ibid., 98.

16. Freud, *Beyond the Pleasure Principle,* 52.

17. Dawkins, "Selfish Genes and Selfish Memes," 143.

18. Searle, *Mind,* 302–303.

19. Ibid., 81.

THREE   *The Freudian Self*

1. Jung, *Memories, Dreams, Reflections,* 149–150.

2. Ibid., 150.

3. Ibid., 155.

4. Ibid., 168, 156, 157.

5. Karl Lueger quoted in Ian Kershaw, *Hitler: 1889–1936. Hubris* (New York: W. W. Norton, 1999), 35.

6. Freud, *Future of an Illusion,* 6; Spengler, *Decline of the West,* 182.

7. Freud, *Interpretation of Dreams,* 137, 196–197; Freud, *Civilization and Its Discontents,* 61–62.

8. Freud and Bullitt, *Thomas Woodrow Wilson,* 195–196, 71.

9. Nietzsche, *Genealogy of Morals,* 19.

10. Spengler, *Decline of the West,* 250.

11. Spencer, *Data of Ethics,* 188–189.

12. Freud, *Civilization and Its Discontents,* 51.

13. There is a recent English translation of Fichte's *Addresses* by Gregory Moore (Cambridge: Cambridge University Press,

2008), the first in eighty-six years. Quotations are taken from the 1922 translation, as reprinted in 1979.

14. Fichte, *Addresses to the German Nation,* 86.

15. Ibid., 268–269.

16. Spengler, *Decline of the West,* 350, 352–353.

17. Freud, *Civilization and Its Discontents,* 33.

18. *Oxford English Dictionary,* 2nd ed., s.v. "Metaphysics."

19. Spengler, *Decline of the West,* 215.

20. Freud, *Beyond the Pleasure Principle,* 26, 27 (emphasis in original).

21. Ibid., 26–27.

22. Freud, *Civilization and Its Discontents,* 12–13.

FOUR   *Thinking Again*

1. Wilson, *Consilience,* 99; Pinker, *How the Mind Works,* 924–926.

2. Pinker, *How the Mind Works,* 324–327, 456–459.

3. Rene Descartes, *The Method, Meditations, and Philosophy of Descartes,* trans. John Veitch (N.p.: M. Walter Dunne, 1901), 270.

4. Pinker, *How the Mind Works,* 4, 64, 21, 30.

5. Wilson, *On Human Nature,* 201.

6. Psalms 8:4; Freud, *Civilization and Its Discontents,* 21–23.

7. Pinker, *How the Mind Works,* 556, 561.

# BIBLIOGRAPHY

Balthasar, Hans Urs von. *Presence and Thought: An Essay on the Philosophy of Gregory of Nyssa.* Translated by Marc Sebanc. San Francisco: Ignatius, 1995.

Bonhoeffer, Dietrich. *Letters and Papers from Prison.* Enlarged edition. Edited by Eberhard Bethge. New York: Macmillan, 1972.

Comte, Auguste. A *General View of Positivism.* Translated by J. H. Bridges. London: Trübner, 1865.

Damasio, Antonio R. *Descartes' Error: Emotion, Reason, and the Human Brain.* 1994. Reprint, New York: Avon, 1995.

Dawkins, Richard. "Selfish Genes and Selfish Memes." In *The Mind's I: Fantasies and Reflections on Self and Soul,* edited by Douglas R. Hofstadter and Daniel C. Dennett, 124–144. New York: Basic, 1981.

Dennett, Daniel C. *Breaking the Spell: Religion as a Natural Phenom-enon.* New York: Viking, 2006.

Descartes, Rene. *The Method, Meditations, and Philosophy of Des-cartes.* Translated by John Veitch. N.p.: M. Walter Dunne, 1901.

Dugatkin, Lee Alan. *The Altruism Equation: Seven Scientists Search for the Origins of Goodness.* Princeton: Princeton University Press, 2006.

Fichte, Johann Gottlieb. *Addresses to the German Nation.* Translated by R. F. Jones and G. H. Turnbull. 1922. Reprint, Westport, Conn.: Greenwood, 1979.

Freud, Sigmund. *Beyond the Pleasure Principle.* Translated by James Strachey, in collaboration with Anna Freud, assisted by Alix Strachey and Alan Tyson. Vol. 18 of *The Standard Edition of the Complete Psychological Works of Sigmund Freud.* London: Hogarth, 1955.

——. *Civilization and Its Discontents.* Edited and translated by James Strachey. New York: Norton, 1962.

——. *The Future of an Illusion.* Edited and translated by James Strachey. New York: Norton, 1961.

——. *The Interpretation of Dreams.* First Part. Translated by James Strachey, in collaboration with Anna Freud, assisted by Alix Strachey and Alan Tyson. Vol. 6 of *The Standard Edition of the Complete Psychological Works of Sigmund Freud.* London: Hogarth, 1981.

——, and William C. Bullitt. *Thomas Woodrow Wilson: A Psychologi-cal Study.* Boston: Houghton Mifflin, 1967.

Gazzaniga, Michael S. *Human: The Science Behind What Makes Us Unique.* New York: Ecco, 2008.

Grotius, Hugo. A *Literal English Translation of the Latin Text of*

*Hugo Grotius, On the Truth of the Christian Religion.* Translated by Thomas Sedger. [London: Whittaker, 1859.] Reprint, Charleston, S.C.: BiblioBazaar, 2008.

Hofstadter, Douglas R., and Daniel C. Dennett, eds. *The Mind's I: Fantasies and Reflections on Self and Soul.* New York: Basic, 1981.

James, William. *The Varieties of Religious Experience: A Study in Human Nature.* 1902. Reprint, New York: Collier, 1961.

———. *The Will to Believe and Other Essays in Popular Philosophy.* 1897. Reprint, Cambridge, Mass.: Harvard University Press, 1979.

Jung, C. G. *Memories, Dreams, Reflections.* Revised edition. Edited by Aniela Jaffe. Translated by Richard and Clara Winston. New York: Pantheon, 1973.

Kugel, James L. *How to Read the Bible: A Guide to Scripture, Then and Now.* New York: Free Press, 2007.

Lueger, Karl. Quoted in Ian Kershaw, *Hitler: 1889–1936. Hubris.* New York: W. W. Norton, 1999.

Nietzsche, Friedrich. *On the Genealogy of Morals: A Polemic.* Translated by Douglas Smith. 1996. Reprint, Oxford: Oxford University Press, 2008.

Pinker, Steven. *The Blank Slate: The Modern Denial of Human Nature.* New York: Viking, 2002.

Pinker, Steven. *How the Mind Works.* New York: W. W. Norton, 2009.

Rorty, Richard, and Gianni Vattimo. *The Future of Religion.* Edited by Santiago Zabala. New York: Columbia University Press, 2005.

Russell, Bertrand. *The Analysis of Mind.* 1921. Reprint, London: George Allen & Unwin, 1933.

———. *Why I Am Not a Christian and Other Essays on Religion and Related Subjects.* London: George Allen & Unwin, 1957.

Searle, John R. *Mind: A Brief Introduction.* New York: Oxford University Press, 2004.

Spencer, Herbert. *The Data of Ethics.* New York: D. Appleton, 1879.

Spengler, Oswald. *The Decline of the West.* Abridged edition. Translated by H. Stuart Hughes. Oxford: Oxford University Press, 1991.

Wilson, Edward O. *Consilience: The Unity of Knowledge.* New York: Knopf, 1998.

——. *On Human Nature.* Cambridge, Mass.: Harvard University Press, 1978.